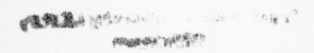

Mark Van Doren: Three Plays

Mark Van Doren:

Three Plays

 HILL AND WANG · NEW YORK

Manufactured in the United States of America
by American Book–Stratford Press, Inc.

Contents

NEVER, NEVER ASK HIS NAME

A Play in Three Acts

●

World Premiere, March 24, 1965,
by The Florida State University Theatre
in co-operation with
The Eddie Dowling University
Theater Foundation

LIST OF PERSONS
And Their Relationships

THE FRAILEY HOUSE

PETER FRAILEY
> JEREMIAH HORN, *his father-in-law*
> REBECCA, *his mother*
> JACK, *his son*
> JOSEPHINE, JACK'S *wife*
> ABEL, *their son*
> DINAH, PETER'S *daughter*
> RUTH, *her child*

THE HARD HOUSE

NATHAN HARD
> ELIZABETH, *his wife*
> ANNA, *a servant*

THE REVEREND AMOS GOLD

Scenes

> *Act One: Living room of* PETER FRAILEY'S *house.*
> *Act Two:*
> > *Living room of* NATHAN HARD'S *house, two hours later.*
> *Act Three:*
> > *Front porch of* PETER FRAILEY'S *house, late afternoon of the same day.*

Time

> *About 1840. New England.*

Act One

Living room of PETER FRAILEY's *farmhouse, one Saturday morning in early fall. A commodious room, not conspicuously well kept, but comfortable like an old shoe; much lived in, with things lying about. At the rear, between two windows, an organ. Doors right and left, both open, leading into other parts of the house.*

JEREMIAH HORN, *old, erect, wearing a short white beard which he frequently smooths with quick hands, bustles in through a door, turning impatiently to gesture at* ABEL *and* RUTH, *cousins of seven and nine, who follow him without fear, as if used to his ways.*

JEREMIAH:

Come on, come on. You children are like flies.
Have to be shooed in, shooed out, shooed off
To other places. Like today. Remember?
We're going to the Hards, and you're not ready.
I told you to be neat and Sunday-dressed:
Shoes clean and faces shining. Abel, Abel,
Look at your shock hair. And Ruth——

RUTH:

                                   Oh, I'm
Not going.

3

JEREMIAH:

   What's this? Not going with your mother?
Poor Dinah, not with her? A whole week there,
And you not helping her to last it out!
Strange enough that she is leaving here—
She never has till now—not since————

  RUTH:

          But I'm

Not going.
Sadly.
  Wish I was.

  JEREMIAH:

       Wish I *were!*

  RUTH:

I wish I *was.* And Mother *wasn't—*
Without me with her, anyway. I'm not
Sup*posed* to go. Grandpa said I wasn't.

  JEREMIAH:

What's this? Where's Peter! Why did he say that?

  RUTH:

I don't know why, Great-grandpa.

  JEREMIAH:

       Ha! Great-grandpa!
Great fiddlesticks! Who taught you to say that?

  RUTH:

You're Grandpa's father.

  JEREMIAH:

      Now, there! Father-in-*law.*
Well! Abel, do you know things like your cousin?
Who do *you* say I am?

   ABEL, *not listening, has gone over to the organ.*
      Now none of that,

My boy. No music, please. Let there be one
Still morning in this house: no wheeze, no whining.

ABEL, *reluctantly, steps away.*

Good boy.

RUTH:

I like it. Abel's a good player.
I listen to him every day, almost.
He plays, and Mother sings. There is one song
Especially——

JEREMIAH:

I know, I know. Who doesn't?
But not today. No time. If you must pump,
Do it with water, Abel, not with air.
Go on now. In the kitchen. Let me hear
Loud splashing. And remember, comb that last
Year's bird's nest there on top of you.

RUTH:

Intercepting ABEL *as he starts out.*

Raccoons
Are little bears. I found it in the book.
The capital of Delaware is Dover—
I found that too.

ABEL:

What book?

RUTH:

The one upstairs,
Outside of Grandma Frailey's room—you know,
The one Aunt Jophy bought from that old peddler.

ABEL:

So you know everything—

Grins.

you think.

JEREMIAH:

Patiently, as ABEL *at last goes out.*

Now, child,
What's this again—not going? Who did you say——

RUTH:

Why, Grandpa did. He said I wasn't to go
And make it any harder.

JEREMIAH:

Harder for him,
He meant, and—well, no wonder. What he knows
Is more than he'll be able to say there.

Pauses, realizing that she doesn't understand.

But how can your sweet mother draw a breath
Without you there to tell her when she may?
Two girls together—ha, that's how it goes.
When have you ever been apart?

RUTH:

Suddenly in tears.

I told him,
Never.

JEREMIAH:

There! O Lord, I made you cry.
You told him, did you, and he didn't listen?
I'll make him listen.

Looks right, left, and shouts.

Peter! Where are *you!*

Waits; no answer.

Now don't you worry, great-granddaughter Ruth.

RUTH:

Laughs as suddenly as she had wept.

That makes me sound so old—as if I'd been here
Ages and ages before Abel was.

JEREMIAH:

Oho!

RUTH:

Two years!

JEREMIAH:

As if that's anything.

RUTH:

It is, it is!

JEREMIAH:

But what I meant to say—
You're going with your mother. Mrs. Hard
Was good enough to ask us all to bring you.
Think of it, this houseful! But the Fair
Took Uncle William and Aunt Bessie off
At daybreak, with your cousins—all but Abel——

RUTH:

Adam took his whistle.

JEREMIAH:

What?

RUTH:

His silver
Whistle, that he got for his birthday.
Grandma Frailey hid it, but he looked
And looked, and there it was, in the same drawer
She keeps her thimble in, and the sharp shears
She won't let Abbie or me or Debbie touch.

JEREMIAH:

Wisely, too. But a whistle—I don't see——

RUTH:

She said it hurt her ears. Then Adam found it,
And blew so loud—oh, it hurt all our ears.

Uncle William thought it would scare the horses,
But I don't think it did. They trotted off
Gentle as pie. I watched them to the bridge.
The last thing we heard, though, was that whistle.
Mother was listening; she likes it loud;
Nothing hurts *her* ears.

    JEREMIAH:

                    She doesn't listen
To most things.

    As if he had never been interrupted.

                Uncle Arthur, too, and Owen—
They've all gone to the Fair. So few at best
Will be there in that cold, hard house. You'll see.

    She shakes her head, not comprehending.

Look sharp, and you will understand. Or will you?

    She shakes her head again.

Of course not. I'm a fool. Oh, dear, oh, dear,

    To himself, but she listens.

What death can do to people life will do,
If lengthened. I forget she is a child.
I always do. The rest of them I don't—

    Voices at the door.

No, not this other one. Good morning, Dinah.

    DINAH *and* REBECCA *come in together.* DINAH, *twenty-seven,
is very thin and pale, and walks as if she did not see well, or
as if she had no clear notion where she was. Once pretty, now
haunted and abstracted, she lets her grandmother lead her to
a small sofa facing the audience and arrange its pillows for
her comfort. Her eyes are mostly on the floor, though whenever anyone speaks they turn slyly in that direction; but not
as if she heard the words.* REBECCA *is tall, gaunt, and bony,
with a tenderness in her face reserved for* DINAH *and her
daughter. She nods at* RUTH, *who flies at once to help.*

RUTH:

Here, Mother, is the small one for your back.

Adjusts pillow.

You love it. It's the one Aunt Jophy made.

Kisses DINAH, *who smiles and touches her, then withdraws her hand.*

You mustn't get tired out before your trip.
Just think, a trip! White horses all the way—
This house and that—you'll pass the school, too,
But this is Saturday, so there's no school—
This barn, that barn—the little ones, the big ones—
Then there you are!

REBECCA:

　　　　　　Don't speak of it too soon,
My dear.

JEREMIAH:

　　　　That's right. Don't agitate her. Becky,
How are those old bones today?

She dismisses the question with a downward wave.

　　　　　　　　No bones?
Mine managed one more night. Oh, dear, these bones.
I didn't use to know I had them. Now
There's nothing else. A man's a bag of bones
And what besides? Oh, yes, a tired mind.
But a busy tongue!

REBECCA:

Without glancing his way.

　　　　　　Busy? So's a bee.

But he has turned and seen a man and woman passing one of the windows.

JEREMIAH:

Here's Jack, here's Josephine. I hope he's hitched
The horses up. Jack is so forgetful.

JOSEPHINE, *handsome, with black hair, comes in with* JACK *behind her, holding* ABEL *by the hand;* ABEL's *hair is plastered down except for a cowlick that sticks out in back.*

JACK:

That's right, Grandpa, I have. They're combed and curried,
Too, and itching to go. They're stomping flies—
September flies, the big ones. You folks ready?
Billy and Dan won't wait—I mean, forever.
Remember that time they ran away?
My fault, of course. I got to talking cheese
With the Boston man that makes pineapple molds—
I said they were too dear, I wouldn't buy—
And what did Dan and Billy do but break
Their hitching straps and light right out for home?
I never did catch up with them. Well—ready?

JOSEPHINE:

Has gone to straighten the folds of DINAH's *long skirt, and pat her hair into better shape.*

Don't hurry people, Jack.

To the others.

To hear him talk,
You wouldn't think he had forgotten us—
Forgotten everything—that we were going——

JACK:

She's right, I did. And you know why? Two things.
Work to do this morning—plenty of it—
Three cows about to calve, and that wet hay
On the side hill—it needs a good tossing,
And even then I wonder if it won't spoil—
And now this visit. Why should we *all* go?
I see no sense in that.

JOSEPHINE:

He sees no sense
In anything he didn't plan himself.

JACK:

Laughs heartily.

She's right, I don't. Abel, you missed a place.

Pulls hard at the cowlick. ABEL, *jerking himself free, goes to the organ and climbs up to it, tentatively fingering the keys.* RUTH *follows and stands beside him.*

RUTH:

Touches ABEL'S *cowlick;* ABEL, *absorbed, pulls away.*

He isn't watching now, so we could play—
I mean, you could.

ABEL *gives no sign that he hears this.*

     Sometime I'm going to learn.
It looks so easy when you do it, Abel.

ABEL:

Not so easy. You can make mistakes.

RUTH:

Or *it* can.

Patting the organ.

   Contrary, I suppose.
A cowlick's contrary—

Touches it again.

     —on a boy.
Girls don't have them. Grandma Frailey, though—
She says we do; only they don't matter.

Runs her fingers back over her ears.

Long hair's a nuisance otherwise.

JOSEPHINE:

To no one in particular.

Jack seems to think Dinah should go alone—
With him of course to drive. He doesn't know
The rest of us are needed to make old Nathan
Miserable.

Rebecca *looks squarely at her.* Jeremiah, *who has started pacing the floor, stops suddenly without turning around. Through the ensuing dialogue he maintains a shocked silence.*

Yes, miserable. Old Nathan—
What does he hate most? Why, all of us know:
A family, a big family. Three's a crowd
For Nathan. Well, we're half a dozen more.
It's all to rub it in. As if he wouldn't
Have had one if he could—the biggest family
Ever. But he hasn't, so he hates us—
Hates Papa, his old neighbor—hates us all——

Rebecca:

Jophy!

Josephine:

What is it, Grandma? Am I wrong?

Rebecca:

You are, to have no feeling for this man
Who had one son and lost him. David died
Ten years ago—count up—exactly ten—

Counts on her fingers.

And that might be enough for most of us
To say it had to be, so let it be.
Not so for Nathan Hard. He can't forget
One bit of it.

Josephine:

One bitter bit.

Rebecca:

You're heartless.
Perhaps he should accept it, but who judges?
His only son—no other child—crushed
In the woods there, beside the waterfall,
When a great rock came rolling down—oh, dear,
I saw the poor boy's body. All of us did;
You did.

JOSEPHINE:

No, I was having my dead baby.

JACK:

She's right. That was the time.

JOSEPHINE:

And maybe you think
I wasn't hurt by that. But I got over it.
We all get over things. We have to, Grandma.

REBECCA:

But Nathan hasn't. And who are we to say—
A handsome, loving son, that might have been——

JOSEPHINE:

Now there! Who knows what David might have been?

REBECCA:

You seem to know yourself. A David worse,
Not better.

JOSEPHINE:

No, not that. Who wouldn't wish
The best luck to anybody alive?
Dead, though, and mouldering in his grave——

REBECCA:

Jophy, how you talk!

JOSEPHINE:

I only say
What anybody might.

REBECCA:

Shakes her head.

Somebody mightn't.
Don't presume, Josephine, too much
On what you have a right to call your honesty.
We're proud of that, but don't you be. A little

Doubt of it is better. Think of Abel,
The only child *you* have. Not nineteen yet,
As David was, but surely you have dreams——

JOSEPHINE:

And keep them to myself. Nor would I envy
Bessie if Abel died, as Nathan envies
Bessie and me our young ones. Even Dinah—
For all I know he hates her having Ruth.
Why shouldn't Nathan love it that we have them—
Love it that his friend has five grandchildren,
With more to come when Owen and Arthur marry?
We are a litter, and he loathes litter;
It spoils the pretty neatness of a dream.
Ruth, now—

    Drops her voice a little, but RUTH *turns her head.*

        oh, what untidiness! No father.

RUTH:

Nudges ABEL, *and whispers to him. He pumps at the organ;
opens a stop.*

But I do have a father—far away.

DINAH:

Lifts her head, stares into the audience, listens intently while
ABEL *with one finger plays the first eight notes of "Barbara
Allen," and when he repeats the notes, sings with him to the
end in a high, sweet, sad ballad voice. He plays slowly, so
that every word she sings will be clear. All listen patiently,
as to a song they have heard many times.*

I had a lover long ago,
  No name had he, that lover.
And I will die before it's known—
  Oh, never, never, never.

I have a husband far away,
  My daughter's father, where-O,
My own truelove, so far away,
  So far down there, down there-O.

*As she sings the last line she points to the floor at her feet,
and shudders. While she is doing this,* PETER *comes in, followed by the* REVEREND AMOS GOLD, *a strict, ascetic, but not
unkindly man of middle age whose dress—a long black coat
and a clean white stock folded neatly, high on his neck—is
old-fashioned compared with that of the others.* PETER *has a
large brown beard; he is uneasy and preoccupied, and never
is unaware of* AMOS's *presence in the room, though* AMOS
*goes almost at once to stand by himself and watch the others,
who evidently are so accustomed to him that they carry on
at first as if he were not there. Only* RUTH *makes any special
gesture: a private one, to* ABEL. *She puts on a pious look and
presses her hands together, pointed up.* ABEL *grins briefly,
then shakes his head as if to rebuke her irreverence.*

PETER:

Here's Reverend, come to see how all of us are.
Sit down, Amos.

Points to a chair.

But I know you won't.
Avenging angels never bend their knees;
Some say they haven't any.

AMOS:

Unsmiling, in a deep voice.

By the throne
Of God—that's true—no angel sits.
But I'm not there, and I am not an angel.
Avenging? That's for those who know the truth,
The whole truth, and nothing but the truth,
And so can judge.

PETER:

Motionless for a moment, looking down where DINAH *continues to point.*

Judge.

Recovers himself, then crosses rapidly to DINAH, *kissing her
cheeks and hair.*

We heard you, Dinah,
Happily. Go on. Abel, some more.

> ABEL *remains motionless at the organ.* PETER, *glancing toward* AMOS, *continues, but as one forcing himself to speak, with only half of his attention on what he says.*

Everything in the world is well, my daughter,
When you consent to sing. What is man's life
If music does not grace it? A mean thing,
I tell you. I am fifty, and I should know.

> *Caresses his beard.*

Now that's not old, Mother,

> REBECCA *shakes her head, slowly.*

                   but it's enough.
When Patience left me seven years ago—
So suddenly was gone—I couldn't bear
A single voice raised then to comfort me:
Your own, or Father Horn's, or in the church
That day the anthem—all those lusty voices
Delighting, so I thought, in their proud selves.
O, Patience, I was wrong. It was for you
They sang, and I sealed my ears. I wanted silence,
Silence.

> *Suddenly becomes silent himself.*

      Well,

> *With a poor attempt at briskness.*

                there's been too much of that.
Dinah, my only daughter, my first child,
Give me this comfort. Sing. Abel, some more.

> *But* DINAH *has dropped her eyes and turned away, and* ABEL, *watching her, now slips off the seat and goes to stand by* JACK. RUTH *goes to* DINAH *and lightly strokes her hands, that lie in her lap.*

I see. Well, Father Horn, they disobey me,
And that is the lot of parents who insist
Too rashly.

JEREMIAH:
>   Don't I know that? Nevertheless
Our lot is to insist. I do it, Peter,
Even with you.

PETER:
Nervously.
>   What now?

JEREMIAH:
>   Oh, nothing, nothing—
Yet.

PETER:
Nodding toward the children.

I should have waited, and I will,
Until the spirit pricks them—if it does.

JEREMIAH:
Waving.

Good morning, Amos.

RUTH:
Bravely.
>   Good morning, Reverend Gold.

AMOS:
Good morning, Mr. Horn. Good morning, Ruth.

RUTH, *pleased at having got his attention, turns back to* ABEL.

JEREMIAH:
Now since you have that house all to yourself—
No wife, no flock of your own—shepherd to others
Only—and mind you, we are grateful—

AMOS *smiles soberly, and bows a little.*
>   Amos,
The bachelors of God cannot conceive
How men of earth suffer.

Turns to Peter.

It's the day,
Peter, and where they're going. They've remembered—
Or Dinah has—the trip they are to take.
Ruth, too—or is Ruth going?

Peter:

Ruth? Why, yes.

Ruth:
Running to him.

Grandpa! You said I couldn't.

Peter:

So I did.
But Mrs. Hard——

Ruth:
Running back to Dinah.

Oh, Mother, after all!
To think of you without me over there.
You need me, don't you? Here!

Pats a pillow. Dinah *accepts the attention, vaguely.*

Jeremiah:
Nodding sententiously.

Peter is wise.

Peter:
Ignoring the old man, turns to the rest.

At any rate, we all of us are going;
Or nearly all.

Looks significantly at Jeremiah, *who straightens himself up
as if resisting the suggestion that he will be left behind.*

Josephine:

Some might suppose I shouldn't.
Some think I try to be the mistress here.

I don't—for Heaven's sake, who'd want to be?
But Grandpa Horn was angry at what I said,
And so was Grandma Frailey; she was the one
That scolded most about it. He was speechless.

PETER:

Now what was that?

She shakes her head, intimating that nobody will tell him.

JEREMIAH:

Peter, you should have been here.
Perhaps she wasn't serious, but she said—
Rebuke me, Josephine, if I belie you
Before this judge

Waving toward AMOS.

who says he is no judge—
She said we all were going to torment him.

PETER:

Agitated.

Torment him? Who?

JEREMIAH:

Why, Nathan. You know who.

PETER:

Anxious.

But how?

JEREMIAH:

By rubbing it in—her word, her word—
That he is childless when we have so many.
She even said he hated us because—
Hated *you* because of David's death—

PETER *stares at him so intently, so strickenly, with a motion of his hand beseeching silence, that he hastens to explain.*

I mean, because *you* suffered no such loss,
And so confront him every day with these.

    Waves around the room.

As if he ever saw us, year on year.
He is a lonely man, God knows; but who
Despises him for that?

    PETER:

                Despises!

    JEREMIAH:

                     Ah,

Not me, not you.

    PETER:

    Painfully, as if pulling himself out of a reverie.

             Oh, certainly not me.

    Searches for something to say; never conquers his confusion.

I thought to save him, not to salt his wounds.
Ten years of mourning—that is overmuch,
Elizabeth, I take it, tells him. Not that I——

    REBECCA:

Nor I. That's Nathan's business.

    PETER:

              So it is.

But now some news she heard last week of Dinah,
Whatever that news was, disturbed her so,
She had to be our neighbor in the end
Despite his prohibition: had to see,
Hear, know, and speak, and God in His goodness willing,

    Glances at AMOS, *who is listening carefully.*

Comfort. That's Elizabeth. And who
Are we to be ungracious? Yet I doubted,
Even then, that I knew what to do.

Perhaps it would be painful if we went.
And still it may be.

Pauses.

May be.

Pauses again.

       I was wrong
To hesitate, however.

JEREMIAH:

      Wrong, Peter?
Natural, I think. It won't be easy
For any of us today.

PETER:

Turns and walks to the window.

       But now the Fair—

Takes out a big silver watch and consults it, relieved at this chance to change the subject.

The horse races! Jack, you're missing those.

JACK:

That's right, I am.

JOSEPHINE:

     He doesn't care too much.

JACK:

Oh, no? What makes you say that? Runners, trotters—
I like the trotters best: the way they come,
All champions if they could be, round the curve,
Then straightaway to where the judges stand,
As if they knew which ones of them *were* judges.
They'd die to please them. Horses are like that.
And I've been told of new ones, sent this year
From over Hartford way: a spotted gelding,

And two black Morgan fillies—keep your eye
On those, Tom Buckley says. Well, Tom,
   Resigned.

                                    you do it,
I can't.

PETER:
      You have your own great team to drive,
With us behind it.

JEREMIAH:
             We'll imagine, Jack,
The road's a racecourse, and the crowds are there—
But don't you really race! We'll just imagine—
Ha! We're winning!
> *Gestures with his hands, as if they held reins.* PETER, *frowning, consults his watch again, then snaps it shut and returns it to his pocket.*

PETER:
           Children, big and little,
Go to the kitchen—off with you—and forage.
If you're not hungry, make yourselves eat something
To stay you until dark when we come home.
No starving, either way. Elizabeth
Said nothing on this subject, so be safe,
I say, instead of sorry. Off with you!
Amos, you go too.

AMOS:
   Not moving, as RUTH, *restless, expects him to.*
          No, I'm not hungry.
I'll stay with you a little if I may.

PETER:
   Uneasy.
You came to see *me?*
   Trying to be light.
          What have I done now?

AMOS:

I came to see you all. I like to come.
This is a happy house,

All look at him, pondering his words.

                        as Nathan Hard's
Is not.

PETER:

   We hope ours is.

Remembers what he was saying.

                    Children, off!

RUTH:

Skips across the room.

Abel, if there's a wishbone, and I think
There is, let's pull it. But you always get
The bigger piece—I don't see how you manage——

ABEL:

Oh, no, you do.

RUTH:

              I did once.

ABEL:

                  Over and over!

RUTH:

Well, anyway, come on.

Stands quietly a few seconds.

               What shall I wish?

She returns across the room to help REBECCA *lead* DINAH *out, followed by* ABEL, *who as he passes the organ runs a hand quietly over the keys.* JEREMIAH, *watching* PETER *closely, makes no move to leave.* JACK *has beckoned to* JOSEPHINE, *but she addresses* PETER.

JOSEPHINE:

Who ever knows for sure what he is doing?
How can we know what deep thing we disturb
Today in that cold house? What dangerous thing?

PETER:

Almost jumps.

Dangerous? Oh, no.

JACK:

               Jophy, I didn't—
You know I didn't—mean as much as that.

JOSEPHINE:

Of course you didn't. I simply took my way—
A long way around, I will admit—
Of saying you were right.

JACK:

Laughing.

               For once, for once.

JOSEPHINE:

And if I went too far——

PETER:

               You did, my dear.
But so do we all.

Glancing at AMOS.

           Go on now, as I said.

Motions for them to follow the others, and they do, JACK
leaving ahead of JOSEPHINE, *who turns back to see if* JERE-
MIAH *is coming too. But* JEREMIAH *has never changed his
position across from* PETER *and* AMOS.

Amos, please.

AMOS:

Shaking his head.

         The church mouse had his fill
This morning.

Looks from PETER *to* JEREMIAH.

         But if you two have a secret——

PETER *starts to gesture in the negative, then stops, his hand
stationary, thinking.*

JEREMIAH:

Secret? That all depends on how he means
To tell me I'm not going with the rest.
At least I think he plans to tell me that.
The secret, Amos, is what *I* intend.

    To PETER.

Peter, I'm going with you.

PETER:

               But you aren't.

JEREMIAH:

Ha! There it is. You're telling me at last.
I knew you were against me, but you waited——

PETER:

Against you? Only this—but you know my reason.

JEREMIAH:

Ha! Your reason? No, Peter, I don't.

PETER:

It's bad enough that Josephine is going.
She can't hold her tongue. But if Jack goes,
She goes; no helping that.

JEREMIAH:

             And you don't trust
Your father-in-law to hold *his* tongue. I see.

PETER:

Not about the one thing you know
And Nathan doesn't. Nathan must never know.
The song Dinah sings—it mustn't mean
To others what it means to you and me.

JEREMIAH:

But she won't sing it there.

PETER:

               Can we be sure?
Josephine—I heard her—forced it out.
"No father." It was like a trigger pulled.

JEREMIAH:

No father. Well, who thinks there is one? Dinah's
Branded.

PETER:

     There you go now. Words like that!

AMOS:

A cruel word indeed. No, Jeremiah.

JEREMIAH:

Impatiently.

I won't use any such in Nathan's house.

PETER:

No words at all. You won't be there.

JEREMIAH:

                I will!
Peter, be the head of your own house
But not the tyrant.

PETER:

         Words again!

JEREMIAH:

What else?
And petty, too. A patriarch at fifty—
That's too soon. Oh, I remember well
How it began. All of your grandchildren
Must have old Bible names: Adam, Abel,
Abigail, Deborah, Ruth. In your own time
You skipped them. You and Patience were content,
Or *you* were, with William, Owen, Arthur——

PETER:

Don't forget our first one. Dinah was named
For Jacob's daughter by Leah, whom his sons
In anger killed a whole great city for.

JEREMIAH:

A rough time *she* had. That's very true.

PETER:

Do not remind me.

JEREMIAH:

Patience, my own daughter—
What did you do to her?

PETER:

How now! What's this?

JEREMIAH:

What did you do but kill *her?*

PETER:

Oh, my God!

AMOS:

Brethren, brethren! I see I shouldn't have stayed.

Starts toward the door.

PETER:

Angrily.

No, Amos, you must hear the end of this,
No matter how the old man raves. *Killed* her!

JEREMIAH:

Five children in five years. You didn't spare
My daughter, did you, Peter? She wore out
When still she was a girl. I'm glad her mother
Died before she saw it.

PETER:

Oh, my God!
You don't know how I loved her.

JEREMIAH:

Yes, I do.
You loved her into the grave.

PETER:

That settles it.
Your tongue has to be tethered. For a moment
I weakened; was about to take you too.
Now never.

JEREMIAH:

Lest I say to Nathan—what?

PETER:

You know as well as I do: the one thing
Nathan must never know. His precious son,
His perfect boy, his David, was Ruth's father.

Suddenly remembering AMOS, *and turning to him.*

There, now! It's out!

AMOS:

Recovering slowly from his astonishment.

I wasn't listening,

If you would have it so. I mean to say,
The secret is still yours.
  Wrings his hands.
      David! Dinah!

JEREMIAH:

Yes, yes. I learned it when you learned it, Peter.
You found her weeping in the woods that day,
And made her tell you; on her knees she did,
And you knelt with her as I happened by.

PETER:

Happened by. You always were everywhere.

JEREMIAH:

I heard you groaning, and I came to help;
And only then I heard——

PETER:

      I know, I know.
Be silent, can't you?

JEREMIAH:

    Haven't I always been?

PETER:

You have, it's true. But something now is different.
The lid is being pried off of our secret;
I pried it off myself, just now.
  Turning his head.
       Amos,
It is your secret now, to keep as we do.

AMOS:

So I said. And promise.

PETER:

      What was the good
Of telling you? I didn't mean to, Amos.

And now you have a sore in your own heart
To thank me for.

PETER:

AMOS:

Touching his breast.

                This heart is not my own.
It is for all to use, and fill as they please
With sadness, sadness.

     Wrings his hands again.

                   But that girl! That boy!

PETER:

To JEREMIAH.

Our secret's safe with him, however unwise
I was to let it out.

JEREMIAH:

              Oh, I trust Amos.

PETER:

But something, let me say again, is different.

     Pauses, then goes on, half to himself.

I don't know how or why, but things have changed;
I trust nobody now.

JEREMIAH:

              Not even yourself?

PETER:

Looks at him sharply; hesitates.

I do, but have to be careful.

JEREMIAH:

               I could watch
And warn you.

PETER:

           Can the kettle save the pot?

JEREMIAH:

Ha! We blacken bravely, you and I.
Yet we're not devils. All we have is knowledge
Of who Ruth's father was. Let's hug it to us
As if we were one man, one friend of Nathan.

PETER:

Yet we're *not* one, not now. We don't see eye
To eye, about ourselves or Nathan either.
I don't know what's got in you——

JEREMIAH:

                       Ha! You took
Those words out of my mouth.

PETER:

                      Well, you stay here.

JEREMIAH:

No!

PETER:

Yes! Let there be no more words—
Your own or mine.

JEREMIAH:

With a gesture of disgust.

                    You want the last one, Peter,
And have it; and I hope it gives you pleasure,
Like the last dollar that a miser counts:
An empty pleasure, being useless gold.

PETER:

Consider, Father Horn,

     More gently, having prevailed.

                this consequence—
A likely one, I think, if Nathan knew:
That he would claim her.

JEREMIAH:

                  Dinah?

PETER:

                  I mean Ruth.

JEREMIAH:

Fantastic, Peter. He would want no witness
Of the unthinkable fact. David would die
Twice over then: henceforth an evil dream
He never could shake off—not like the one
He's lived in, oh, not like that dream at all,
Bad as it is. He has never forgiven God
For snatching his boy away.

PETER:
Slowly.

                  Then it was God?

JEREMIAH:

Who else?

PETER:

Silent a few seconds; looks at AMOS.

         Why, no one, surely. Yes—who else?

JEREMIAH:

You say it coldly——

PETER:

             No——

JEREMIAH:

              As if you felt
No pity for your old friend who is childless——

PETER:

Childless——

JEREMIAH:

Even though the one he had——

PETER:

Even though——

JEREMIAH:

Has been watching him closely.

Peter, I misjudged you.
How could I have said it—cold? You feel
As I do, whatever David did.
That day, with Dinah weeping in the woods,
We both of us thought death too good for him.

> *Looks to see if* PETER *agrees, but there is no response except*
> *from* AMOS, *who moves so that he can look squarely into*
> PETER's *face, and moves again when* PETER *turns away.*

Yet when it came—ah, things were different then.
We hadn't thought of Nathan, or Elizabeth—
No, or even of David. Only Dinah.
And terrible that was—and is—and will be
Till death lays all of us down so we can sleep
And sleep as if no world had ever been:
No night, no day, no sickness, wellness, nothing.
Ah, it is different when strangers weep;
And as for friends—what can we do but cry
As they do, losing a thing as precious
As he was to them? And all the worse
If we must know something they never will;
If it is here between us, so that tears
Are dryer in our eyes—thinking, thinking—
Than in their own, that merely feel and feel.
I know you feel as I do; so forgive me
The doubts of it I had. You made me angry,
Peter, and so I struck at you—struck twice—
At Patience, too. Forgive me.

PETER *nods, slowly.*

That was wild,
And now I wince, remembering. Forgive me——

PETER:

Impatiently.

No need, no need——

JEREMIAH:

As we have forgiven David.

PETER *nods almost imperceptibly.*

But Nathan hasn't made his peace with God.
Poor man, I pity him; and know you do.
Go with my blessing. Comfort whom you can.

Turns.

Amos, I cannot be sorry now
That you stayed with us, heard us. It's a burden
Both of us have borne too long, too long.

AMOS:

And in His silence

Spreads both hands upwards.

I can help you bear it.
For purposes like this I was ordained.
I pity all of you, in both your houses,
But shall not shout it out. So have no fear.

JEREMIAH:

The fear is not for us. It is for Nathan.

AMOS:

You speak nobly. Let him rest. And yet
There are some hidden things here still to fear.
The secret—

Looks calmly at PETER.

—have I all of it?

PETER:

Startled.

What's that?

AMOS:

Is there no more to learn? Not that I ask.
In God's good time I'll learn; we all shall learn.

PETER:

Reverend! What are you saying?

AMOS:

I am saying
The pity of it goes so deep, my friend,
That I have not touched bottom. When I do,
It will be you that tells me I am there.

Starts out of the room.

PETER:

Running to catch his arm, but failing.

Reverend! Reverend!

AMOS *disappears through the door.*

JEREMIAH:

Reverend Amos Gold!

Shaking his head.

He's taking on himself a bit too much.
As if we hadn't told him all we could!
You did, I know—unwisely. Yes, Peter.
Unwisely.

PETER:

Staring after AMOS.

Let it be.

JEREMIAH:

Oh, it must be.
A silence, broken, cannot hush again.

PETER:

With a loud, involuntary sigh.

No, never.

JEREMIAH:

And it may be just as well.

Noise offstage of the children returning.

So, Peter, it is time. God go with you.

Curtain.

Act Two

Living room of NATHAN HARD'S *farmhouse, two hours later.*
Commodious, like PETER'S, *but more expensively furnished,*
and perfect in its order, suggesting that fewer persons use it.
There is only one door at the side, for this is a wing. The
furniture includes two long sofas and several large, deep
chairs. Against the wall opposite the door, a low piano of
highly polished dark wood, its keys covered. Over the fire-
place, facing the audience, a long rifle, inlaid with brass,
hangs from two strong silken cords.

ANNA *moves about the room, dusting and straightening ob-*
jects which scarcely need it. She is tall and spare, with stiff
motions and an angular, forbidding face. She does not look
up as ELIZABETH HARD *comes in for a final inspection.* ELIZA-
BETH *is beautiful, fair-haired, and serene, and she makes no*
attempt to look younger than she is—in her late forties.

ANNA:
Still not looking up.
There. This will have to do.

ELIZABETH:
                    It does do, Anna,
Thank you. You're a dear—and don't pretend
You've done it all with your left hand. I know

How early you got up, how well you've worked
To make the house look right for our old friends.

ANNA:

Old friends. I hope I know them when I see them.

ELIZABETH:

Smiles.

Oh, they won't be much changed.

Pauses.

I *think* they won't,
The grown ones at least. The little ones
I've never even seen. Perhaps you have.

ANNA:

Not if you haven't.

ELIZABETH:

Anna! I never said——

ANNA:

You never did. But don't I know my duty?
By Mr. Hard, I mean.

ELIZABETH:

Oh, Anna, Anna,
Don't say that.

ANNA, *silent, stoops to rearrange a small rug.*

Whatever he desires,
Or doesn't, you are free—you always have been,
Ever since you started with us here,
The first day we walked into this house——

ANNA:

I know it, Mrs. Hard. It's my house too.

ELIZABETH:

Of course it is.

ANNA:

> And so are all its troubles,
Passing and to come.

ELIZABETH:

> No more to come.
Please think of it that way.

Clasps her hands.

> Oh, it's so good
To be expecting company—and of all people,
These. Old Mrs. Frailey, and Mr. Horn—
Not them, I understand, but most of the others.

ANNA:

Some of them went to the Fair.

ELIZABETH:

> Yes, William's family.
But Dinah and her father—those are the ones
I chiefly mean. Dinah—that poor girl.

ANNA:

It all depends.

ELIZABETH:

> No, it doesn't, Anna.
Mr. Frailey, too.

ANNA:

Looks straight at her for the first time.

> *That* all depends.

ELIZABETH:

Oh, not so much. I've pitied the poor man so.
His daughter, then his wife.

ANNA:

> She's really dead.

ELIZABETH:

Anna! Don't you have respect for death?
Goes to stand by the window; looks out, but not to see.

ANNA:

I do. For danger, too.

ELIZABETH:
Turns back.

                          Danger?

ANNA:
Sepulchrally.

                                    Danger.

ELIZABETH:

About to protest, but changes the subject.
I ought to have asked them all for noonday dinner,
And would have, but they might have thought they shouldn't,
And so not come at all.

ANNA:

                          I fixed some things.
I'll have them on the table: cookies, coffee.

ELIZABETH:

I know you did, I saw them. You were wiser——

ANNA:

Never hurts.
Suddenly runs to the door.
                    Reminds me of the oven——
Oh!

Has almost collided with NATHAN, *coming in. Goes out past
him. He does not give her a glance. He is a little shorter than*
PETER, *with white hair immaculately brushed, a ruddy face,
and intense blue eyes, red at the rims, that search out* ELIZA-
BETH *by the window. He has on, obviously, his best clothes,*

though he is uncomfortable in them, as if he had not worn them for years. From time to time he pulls at his shirt collar, too tight about his neck.

NATHAN:

Well, dear, I'm ready.

ELIZABETH:

Nervously, not managing very well a playful curtsey.

Dressed to kill!

NATHAN:

Why not? State visit.

ELIZABETH:

Or a sacrifice.

But let's not call it that.

Hesitates.

I didn't tell you—

Dinah's little girl is coming with her.

NATHAN:

Flushes.

Damnation on disgrace! I told you, Lizzie,
I wouldn't have that bastard in my house—
I'd rather burn it. This is a trick.

ELIZABETH:

Please, Nathan.

NATHAN:

You thought you'd wait till it was past the time
To head them off, then tell me. Listen, Lizzie;
There's always time to leave. I'm still no prisoner
In this or any room of any house.

Starts for the door.

Have them to yourself. Say I'm sick

Upstairs. Or no—say I've gone to town
In a locked wagon. The sheriff wants to hang me.

ELIZABETH:
Come back here, Nathan.
She seems to know he will.
It's for David's sake.
He stops dead, but does not turn around.

NATHAN:
David! What do you mean! How do you dare——

ELIZABETH:
He was our boy, and Dinah is Peter's girl.
For all good children's sake——

NATHAN:
Good children!
Lizzie, are you mad?

ELIZABETH:
Ruth, anyway—
How can that child be blamed? So I wrote Peter——

NATHAN:
Peter.
Says it tonelessly.

ELIZABETH:
I told him both should come; the two,
It seems, are seldom separated: paired
In misery, perhaps. Peter was glad.

NATHAN:
He's always been for messes; he would like it.
The more the merrier, buzzing round his head.
A male sow, with millions at the tit.
She gasps.
I'm sorry; that's excessive; but the man
Is wearisome to me.

ELIZABETH:

When have you seen him?

NATHAN:

No matter. Now as to Dinah and this child:
You say misery pairs them. I would say,
Evil is braided in them; strand for strand,
They're tainted.

ELIZABETH:

We'll be seeing for ourselves
If any taint appears.

NATHAN:

If I can look.

ELIZABETH:

Poor Dinah. People say she breaks their hearts.

NATHAN:

You want yours broken—
Clenches his hands.

—again?

ELIZABETH:

Waits.

No, but I'm willing.

NATHAN:

A sacrifice?

ELIZABETH:

A thing I need to do,
For my sake, for David's—don't be angry.
I only mean, as he was ours, so Dinah
Is Peter's, and Ruth is Dinah's: all one chain
Of tenderness, if we pick up the links.
We can, too, after all these years.

NATHAN:

Musing.

Our good,
Our loving boy. He was the whole chain,
And suddenly it parted.

ELIZABETH:

Loving, you say.
I think he still is loving, still desires
That we obey our hearts. So then I say,
For David's sake. David would pity Dinah,
Whatever thing she did, whoever it was
That harmed her—she has never been the same.
I wish he knew, whoever that man was,
Or is, if he still is; I wish *he* knew.

NATHAN:

I wish we still had David. Oh, my God,
I wish we did.

*She drops her hands at her sides, helplessly; the remainder of
his speech is directed to the audience.*

What devil was in that day,
That hour, that minute, second, when the stone
Moved? Why did it have to move? It sat
For centuries; was nothing till that tick
Of time; then everything. I curse it now
As I did then; I never will forgive it.

ELIZABETH:

Nathan——

NATHAN:

Nor God, because He let it go.

ELIZABETH:

Nathan——

NATHAN:

Nor Peter, because he said so little.

I went to him and wept; he saw me, heard me,
And he himself was stone.

ELIZABETH:

Peter was tongue-tied.
So everybody was—Patience—Rebecca——

NATHAN:

But he was Peter, whom I counted on,
Who never yet had failed me. When I said
Such things of David as were deepest here—
My son, my only son, I wept and said,
My one excuse for being, my sole joy—
He listened as to a stranger; looked away;
Was restless till I stopped. Then he said nothing,
Or next to nothing. Peter deserted me.

ELIZABETH:

And you've deserted Peter, he could say:
No pity for his plight. His eldest child,
His only daughter, wrecked upon the shore
Of womanhood.

NATHAN:

Her doing.

ELIZABETH:

Yes, I know,
But wrecked. And Peter sees it every day.
A terrible quiet in her, I have heard.
As if she had been twisted out of speech:
Wrung till she was dry. And little Ruth:
They say she is a merry one at times,
Which makes it all the worse—although I wonder.

NATHAN:

Wonder all you please. But don't forget
The day our light went out—completely out;
No wreckage; nothing, nothing. And the night

We live in is our night alone; nobody
Calls to us, nobody comprehends.

ELIZABETH:

We haven't called to them; except that now
They're coming; they consented.

NATHAN:

                                        Curiosity.

ELIZABETH:

Nathan, no! They hesitated. Peter——

NATHAN:

Still tongue-tied? I doubt it.

ELIZABETH:

                              No, concerned
For Dinah's peace of spirit, that a change
Might shatter.

NATHAN:

                    So with me. Remember, Lizzie,
How utterly I wait here in the dark
For my own end.

ELIZABETH:

                    Nathan, you dote on death.

NATHAN:

I died when he did, for he was my life.

ELIZABETH:

I wasn't, even a little? You were mine,
As he was, till he went; then you were all—
Are all. Look at me, Nathan. I am here—
Your wife, not widow—with you in the dark,
If dark must be; but in the light, if daylight——

NATHAN:

He was my life, I say. And you were too
When you kept quiet with me; when you listened,

As I did, to the last sound of him, leaving:
A door that softly closed; he was considerate,
He shielded us, he thought. Oh, David, no.
It was a thousand thunders, deafening me;
Your mother, though, after enough of time,
Hears outer voices, and betrays to them
Our deep, unspeakable secret.

    ELIZABETH:

                        For his sake,
I said, not mine or yours.

    NATHAN:

                      Oh, heresy
For which men used to burn: claiming to know
In their own hearts the purpose of the world,
And for whose sake they sinned.

    ELIZABETH:

                     Nathan—forgive me—
One thing I think I know, and I must say it.
It was not you that died when David did,
But time. For you, I mean, and only you.
Time died, and that was what put out the light.
Change never breathed again; the very breath
Of being stopped; things stood there in the dark
Like ghosts of their own selves. So David did:
A statue, not a creature; stone, not blood.

    NATHAN:

Stone! Blood!

    ELIZABETH:

                Listen to me, Nathan.
David would have changed as all things do.
For worse, for better— Oh, I think for better.

    NATHAN:

Better!

ELIZABETH:

Even better. But you keep him,
Nathan, as he was; or think you know,
If he had changed, what manner of man now
You'd have in him. And yet a copy still:
More of the sweet same. Whereas——

NATHAN:

More!

No need of any more. He was—
Gropes for a word.

the most.

ELIZABETH:

And saying so, you bind him, press him down
To be what you would have him. But no man
Keeps any other down. Forgive me, Nathan—
This is my worst—you did that while he lived.
You made a mold; demanded that he fill it;
And when he didn't——

NATHAN:

But he always did.

ELIZABETH:

He had to seem to. Nathan, don't you know—
David was afraid of you.

NATHAN:

My God!

*Lifts his hand as if to strike her; holds it there, trembling;
then* ANNA *comes in, glancing behind her through the door.*

ANNA:

They're here.

NATHAN *wheels to the window and pretends to look out.*
ELIZABETH, *after a quick glance at his back, goes swiftly to
the door, through which* JACK *enters first.*

ELIZABETH:

Jack!

Takes both his hands.

You're just the same!

JACK:

Smiles broadly.

And so are you.

ABEL *and* RUTH *walk in together, timidly.*

ELIZABETH:

Now who are these? Don't tell me. This is Ruth.

RUTH *has been turning to look behind her.*

I would have known. She has her mother's eyes—
When I can see them.

Smiles, but when RUTH *turns to look at her, soberly, becomes equally sober, putting out a hand which* RUTH *takes
shyly, looking down.*

And this boy is——

JACK:

Abel.

He's mine. Abel!

ABEL *puts out a hand, awkwardly, and bobs his head.*

ELIZABETH:

Oh! And here *they* are.

JOSEPHINE *leads* DINAH *in, followed by* PETER, *who remains
quietly by the door.*

Josephine,

Kisses her on the cheek.

you haven't turned a hair.
You and Jack are miracles. No change
At all. You've stopped Time in his tracks.

JOSEPHINE:

Well, no.

The old man keeps after me. He's lame,
They say, but he's forever catching up
With some of those that brag of being nimble.
But thank you, Mrs. Hard. This is Dinah.
Can she sit down? She's tired, after the ride.

ELIZABETH:

Hastening to a sofa facing the audience, and plumping the cushions.

I thought she would be, and I've even turned
Her bed down, if she wants to go upstairs.

Hesitates to address her, then does.

Dinah, would you rather——

But stops when it is apparent that DINAH does not know her, does not seem to hear her, and keeps her eyes either down on the floor or across the room on NATHAN's back, which fascinates her as she sinks onto the sofa.

JOSEPHINE:

She misses Grandma.

The two of them are thick as woman thieves—
The worst kind, you know.

JACK:

Edging towards NATHAN.

Jophy's a joker.

Ruth's a third one, then. She sits by Dinah
All day long, to keep herself from mischief.

RUTH *is already by* DINAH's *side.* ABEL, *attracted by the piano, approaches it, one step at a time, until he can lift the lid from the keys and look along the board. Soon, while the conversation proceeds, he climbs onto the seat and runs his fingers right and left without making any sound.*

Mr. Hard, good morning! Or is it noon?

NATHAN:

Without turning, takes out his watch.

Ten minutes to. No, nine and a half.

ELIZABETH:

Leaves DINAH *to go to* PETER, *who has been watching the women, and over their heads,* NATHAN.

                              Peter!
Don't think nobody's noticed you were here.
Hello at last, and welcome.

   They take each other's hands, self-consciously.

                    If I should say
You hadn't changed, would I be telling the truth?

PETER:

Sighs.

You know you wouldn't. Elizabeth, are you well?

ELIZABETH:

With a quick glance toward NATHAN.

We both are well, now that our old friend
Is good enough to come and ask if we are.

JACK:

To NATHAN.

How many horses do you have these days?
I can remember that big team of roans,
But I suppose they're gone.

   NATHAN, *turning halfway, nods.*

                         Billy and Dan,
My dapples—you must see them when we go.
I'm proud of them, but they're a handful too.
Frisky—they would shy at a piece of paper.
But that's all right, the sluggish ones I'll leave
To sluggards. How many horses did you say?

NATHAN:

I didn't say. But sixteen, plugs and all.
I need that many: fourteen for the fields,
And two for driving. But they're never driven.

JACK:

Too bad, too bad. Not good for them.

NATHAN:

Turns fully around.

                              Perhaps.

JACK:

No, certainly. Our neighbor to the south—
You know, Calhoun—foundered his that way:
Fed their idle bellies till they burst.

NATHAN:

Bad management. He was a fool.

JACK:

                         I'll tell him so.

Laughs.

Shall I?

NATHAN:

          Just as you like.

JACK:

                    He's touchy, though.

ELIZABETH:

Has been listening with delight to the sound of their voices.

Nathan, here they are, here all of them are:

NATHAN, *rigid, stares only at her as she gestures.*

Dinah and Ruth, Jack there, and Josephine;
Abel, at the piano—can you play it,
Abel?

Absorbed in the keys, he turns slightly, shaking his head, but then giving it a doubtful nod.

JOSEPHINE:

  Oh, not now.

ELIZABETH:

                And here is Peter.

The two men, facing each other across the room, lift their right hands mechanically. NATHAN remains where he is, but PETER moves slowly behind the others, approaching him.

Anna—you older ones remember Anna—

JACK and JOSEPHINE smile at her, standing near the door, but she keeps her eyes on PETER and NATHAN.

Has things for you to eat and drink, and soon
You must go in with her. If you can stay
For dinner, good; do that.

JOSEPHINE:

                          Oh, thank you. No.
We had a bite at home before we left.
So many of us—we would be like locusts.
We only came to leave *them.*

  Indicating DINAH and RUTH.

PETER:

Reaching NATHAN at last.

                Hello, Nathan.

Neither offers to shake hands.

I trust we're not too many. When we go,
These quiet ones we brought will be, you'll notice,
As if they weren't here. I find them so.
Days pass, and Dinah never speaks a word.
Elizabeth was kind—she always was—
To want them with her.

  Hesitates.

                But if they intrude——

NATHAN:

They don't—for Lizzie. As for me—forget them;
Leave them here. What difference can they make?
Most times I'm elsewhere.

PETER:

            With a farm to run;
I know.

NATHAN:

      You do not know. I have four men,
With families, to do it for me now.
I leave it all to them.

PETER:

         Well, if you can,
You're lucky.

NATHAN:

       I'm not lucky; you know that.
For God's sake—lucky!

*He says this with such vehemence, his voice suddenly rising
in pitch, that* PETER *steps back; and* ELIZABETH *lifts a hand,
gently waving it; but she is ignored.*

       Of all men alive,
The least. And you know why, unless in ten
Long years you've managed somehow to forget.

PETER *shakes his head slowly, fearfully.*

No? Neither have I. How could I? Son
And partner; we'd have had this place together;
And then *he'd* have it—he and his own sons—
My God, forget!

PETER:

      I understand.

NATHAN:

        You don't.

My boy was there that day—why was he there?—
Walking so idly by your waterfall,
So idly—why did you let him trespass, why
Did I not keep him home? But he was young—
Nineteen he was—he liked to walk alone,
And in good time I knew that this would pass—
And then the rock rolled down.

>   *Covers his face.*

PETER:

>   *Waits, then speaks with sudden, desperate resolution.*

                              He wasn't alone.

NATHAN:

>   *Drops his hand.*

What's that? You fool, he was! Unless you mean
Loud water, and his thoughts— O, what those were
I wish I knew—the last thing that he thought,
The very last—I'd write it in black ink,
Then bind it in a book for all to read
Who knew him. But who knew him as I did?

PETER:

>   *Quietly, but with a brooding emphasis.*

We knew him. Some of us more, some of us less.

NATHAN:

But none of you as I did. Every word
He uttered I remember, and keep it here

>   *Strikes his chest.*

In my own book, for no one else to read.

PETER:

>   *As if making up his mind after a long silence.*

Nathan——

NATHAN:

       Be still. Don't lecture me. I grieve
Too much? Is that it, Peter? Only Lizzie
May say those words to me. Not that I listen—
How can I, when the senseless, senseless sound
Of something loosened, something tumbling, something
Meaningless as matter fills my ears
And hurts them, hurts them. Matter! And no mind.
God turned His head that day. He was not there.
How could this be? Better it had been murder,

    PETER *steps farther away.*

And I knew who—oh, then the sweet revenge!
Better it had been malice, with intent
To kill—oh, then my answer!
    Points to the gun.
                    But it was nothing,
Nothing. God was elsewhere. His empty
World it was that did it. Oh, my son,
God murdered you!

    All in the room are motionless, listening. Even DINAH *listens,*
    even RUTH *at her feet; though* RUTH *also watches* ABEL,
    tense at the keys, listening himself as for some signal to play.
    Then without warning he begins. The first eight notes of
    "Barbara Allen" are shrill and clear in the room, startling
    everybody except DINAH, *who leans forward, her hands*
    working in her lap.

JOSEPHINE:

Abel! Don't do that. You're not at home.

ELIZABETH:

Oh, let him! No one plays it any more.
Nathan? You don't mind?

NATHAN:

Aware again of the rest. Shrugs.
              Let the boy play.

ABEL starts again; continues; and DINAH, *sitting straighter, continues with him.*

DINAH:

I had a lover long ago,
   No name had he, that lover.
And I will die before it's known—
   Oh, never, never, never.

I have a husband far away,
   My daughter's father, where-O.
My own truelove, so far away,
   So far down there, down there-O.
   Pauses; and PETER'S *family, assuming she is finished, shift their positions a little.*

JOSEPHINE:

She sings that all the time. We know it by heart.

ELIZABETH:

Is there no more? It's very sweet.

JOSEPHINE:

                   Oh, no,
That's all of it.

NATHAN:
Scornfully.

        No more is needed. The man's
Anonymous, we learn. Well, let him be.
   But DINAH *does not relax. She goes on singing, this time without* ABEL, *who himself sits motionless, listening.*

DINAH:

One father had an only son,
   NATHAN *stares at her.*
   One had a pretty daughter.
And one was cruel, and one was kind
   Until his dear girl wandered.

PETER *turns suddenly, staring too.*

She wandered with that neighbor boy,
   By night, by day she kissed him.
And if I ever say his name,
   In God's name do not listen.

She carried in her then a babe,
   But it would have no father.
He came one day to tell her so,
   Beside the falling water.

NATHAN:

   To PETER—*both of them are strained, intent.*

You said he wasn't alone. Who wasn't alone?
Is it an old song? But the girl is daft.

DINAH:

   As if she had not been interrupted.

She looked on high and saw the stone
   Come tumbling down that killed him.
She looked again, and someone ran:
   Her own dear father, guilty.

PETER:

   Raises both hands in horror; turns to JOSEPHINE.

What has possessed her? Could she make this up?
Is it a new song? Stop her, Abel, stop her.

   JOSEPHINE, *bewildered, touches* DINAH'S *shoulder.* RUTH
   looks steadily at ABEL, *waiting.* PETER *starts toward the
   piano, but stops dead when* NATHAN *calls out in a terrible,
   tortured voice; while* ELIZABETH, *stricken, looks wildly at*
   PETER *and covers her face with her hands.*

NATHAN:

Stop her? No! For God's sake, girl, go on!
However mad it is, we'll hear it out.
Is it mad, Peter? Do you say it is?

PETER:

Without turning his head.

Do you? Have you learned anything? Anonymous!

NATHAN:

Covering his face.

Don't! Don't! I'm staggered.

Drops his hand.

But the girl is foolish.
All of us are imbeciles to heed her.
Lizzie, where have you gone?

ELIZABETH:

Stumbles toward him.

I'm here, I'm coming.
I heard it, Nathan.

Brokenly.

Peter—David—Peter!

NATHAN:

Stay where you are. Nobody move a step.
Go on, girl, go on. We'll hear you out.

DINAH:

Obediently, meekly.

No need had he to roll death down
   Upon her precious lover.
Until she died she never would
   Their secret have discovered.

He was afraid, that slender prince,
   Of his own father's fury.
So he had come to say farewell,
   Farewell to you, my dearest.

PETER *and* NATHAN, *beside themselves, start toward each other, then step apart.*

He would have gone, and none been here
   Except the babe she carried,

To live with her alone, alone,
  Through all the days forever.

JACK:
In a loud voice, laughing nervously.
Sis, where did you find that song? It's new
To me. It's blood and thunder, like in the old
Days, before we came to God's country.

NATHAN:
God's! You mean the fiend's, if this is more
Than madness in that girl.
  Goes over and stands before DINAH, *who never looks up at him.*
                      Listen to me!
What are you getting at, who are you saying
Was father to this child? Fathers, fathers!
Cruel, kind! And one that was afraid—
Don't tell me, girl, there's history in it. No,
It's claptrap, it's balladry.

ANNA:
Screaming out to the audience after a long, watchful silence.
                      It's God's
Own truth. I've known it from the time it happened.
Oh, that it hadn't, but it did. Our boy's
Poor body, bruised. No word of it from him—
He was past talking, David was. But Dinah—
She told me then of how they had been lovers.
So sly, but they were one another's slaves.
Then sudden sickness in her—oh, the terror
Not to be told; except that old man Horn,
He learned of it when Peter Frailey did.
They knew, those two; and one of them came there
The day David died. The song is true.
All of these years it ripened in her head,
Ten long witless years, with no one guessing.
But I knew then. Before his breathing stopped,

And her sweet wit was nipped—oh, frosty death—
She told me; pointed up, the pitiful child,
And told me of the one that ran away.
Her father, Peter Frailey. Here he is,
Among us, live as ever. But he's died
Ten thousand deaths, I know. Mercy on him!

NATHAN:

The rest stand stricken, staring incredulously at PETER, *who stares at nothing visible.*

Anna, are *you* mad?

ANNA:

Mercy upon him!

NATHAN:

For if you're not, Anna, then you've been
A traitor in my kitchen—all these rooms—
All through this house, a serpent, coiled and waiting,
Only to strike now. Oh, not to have told me!

ANNA:

Of what? Of which thing first? For there were two things
I'd rather not have known. It wasn't pleasant,
Knowing. It has spoiled my life for me.

ELIZABETH *turns towards her, pressing her hands together.*

Two things I say. David first—his doings——

NATHAN:

Furious.

Don't touch my son. Don't say his name like that.

ANNA:

You still can't believe it.

NATHAN:

What I do
Or don't believe is not for you to order.

ANNA:

I order nothing. And I never did;
I knew how it would hurt you. It hurt *me*.
Not that it wasn't lovely in itself.
Love, I'm sure, is lovely.

NATHAN:

                              Ears of angels,
Listen and be edified. This witch——

ANNA:

But the dear boy refused to own his act——

NATHAN:

Aha! His act! By God, can no one stop her?

ANNA:

Only by strangling me. But I am finished.
I never meant to tell. It was her song
That did it. Oh, if I hadn't run that day
To help, and heard the wild words she said.

NATHAN:

Wild? Ah, then——

ANNA:

                        No, sir, they were wild
With woe; they weren't false. I am a judge
Of truth, as you are, and I only ask
Which of the two I would have robbed you of:
David, or Peter Frailey? Son, or friend?

NATHAN:

Both of them, you fool. But don't say friend.
    Starts walking past PETER *toward the fireplace, his eyes on
    the gun.*
In his ten years of borrowed time he's been
No friend to me; he never has come near;
Never has uttered even one lying word

Of sorrow for my son. Had he done that—
Well, who's to say an open sore can't close,
No matter what the medicine?

> *Arrives at the mantel; reaches for the gun.* PETER, *as if paralyzed, watches him.*

ELIZABETH:

                    Darling! Don't!
Look round at me. Listen, Nathan! Oh,
Not here, not now—not ever!

NATHAN:

Still with his back to the room.
                              Lizzie, be still.
Let Peter speak. He is the one I wait for—
Have waited for on borrowed time—his time,
That's up today. Not here, not now, but—well,
Peter?

> *Gets the gun in his hands and manipulates its bolt, which makes a loud click; at which all in the room save* DINAH *start in terror.* ANNA, *still by the door, folds her arms and watches.*

PETER:

Hoarsely.
   Listen.

NATHAN:

Wheels about, the gun across his chest.
            I'm listening. Go on.
Tell all the lies you've brooded these long years.

PETER:

No lies. Consider, Nathan, how the truth
Would have sounded on that day, or any day—

NATHAN:

I love the truth.

PETER:

You don't, I think.

NATHAN:

You think,
But you don't know, do you? I love the truth.

PETER:

If I had told it then, and added why—
For that was necessary—you'd have known
Too much for any man. And so I waited
For some more tolerable, more proper time.
Which never came. I've suffered from this too.
I *feared* the truth, the worst of which was what
I did that day.

Shudders.

Yes, I did it, Nathan,
And not one moment since has been my own.
The very clock has been my jailer, ticking
The term of this confinement, with no end
Till now.

Stands more erectly.

And I am happy it has come.
Nor do I hint of mercy. I have suffered—

NATHAN:

Good. I'm glad of it.

PETER:

But think back, Nathan—
Not that I mean to sponge my action out—
To the bad time before, when I first learned—
I loved my daughter too, no less than you
Loved David. You have seen her. She is changed.

NATHAN:

By what you did.

PETER:
> And David before that,
Refusing——

NATHAN:

Trembles, lowers the gun, which still he holds crosswise in front of him.

> Don't touch him! Leave my son
To me. And now get out. All of you—go!
This afternoon, Peter, the clock stops.
Not here, not now, but look for me; and live
Till then. Your debt of time is overdue.

Rushes toward the rest.

Be off, you Fraileys!

> PETER, *as if more fearful for the others than for himself, signals that they should go. He places himself between them and* NATHAN *while they get up in confusion and hurry to the door,* JOSEPHINE *tossing her head as she leads* DINAH. *The children, frightened, run in and out among their elders; though* RUTH *attempts to stay by* DINAH'S *side.* ANNA, *expressionless, continues to watch.*

> Back to your pigsty.

ELIZABETH:

Imploring him with her hands as PETER, *half turning, then resuming his guardian's role, with dignity herds them out.*

Nathan. *They've* done nothing!

JACK:

Reappears in the door, menacingly.

> Mr. Hard,
I know how this has been for you—but look!
You called us——

NATHAN:

> Horses, then, if you prefer.

JOSEPHINE:

Reappears behind JACK, *dragging* ABEL *by one hand.*

A mare, a colt—

Pointing to herself and ABEL.

                              —how kind, how good of you!
It makes us feel much better. I am sure
You want us to feel better, don't you—don't you?

RUTH:

Offstage, her voice raised to reach ABEL.

Abel, those people didn't like that song.
Did you? I did. Oh, Mother, it was lovely.

NATHAN:

Saddle yourselves, by God, and go!

        JACK, JOSEPHINE, ABEL *hesitate, then leave.*

                                        Peter,

Through the door.

Remember. I'll be coming, as I promised—
Me and my friend.

Pats the gun.

ELIZABETH:

Screams.

                    Nathan! Put it back!

NATHAN:

My only friend. It speaks with the tongues of angels—
Nothing but truth. You'll see. I love the truth.

ANNA:

Stationary, with set lips.

I don't. I've lived with it too long. A bitter
Mistress, Mr. Hard. You'll find her so.

                    Curtain.

Act Three

Front porch of PETER'S house, late afternoon of the same day. The roof sags in places; the wooden steps are old and uneven. Several chairs in an irregular row, facing the audience. Door in center, half open. Baskets, tubs, a rake, a hoe, against the house wall. Windows right and left of the door, with drawn curtains. A strip of lawn before the porch, leading either way.

DINAH sits in one of the chairs, staring forward, attentive to nothing visible. RUTH, at her feet, watches ABEL at the end of the porch; he takes first the hoe, then the rake, trying them over his shoulder as if they were guns; selects the rake; brings it forward, thrusting it ahead of him, as at an enemy who threatens.

RUTH:
Grandpa doesn't want us to play with that.
He said so; the teeth are sharp as needles.
He said so.

ABEL:
As if he hadn't heard. Thrusts again, fiercely.
        Don't you come a half inch farther.
Stay there. Now turn around. Now go, now git!

67

RUTH:

If they were Indians would they be afraid
Of such a thing as that?

ABEL:

Indians!

RUTH:

Bows
And arrows would be better—lots of arrows,
Flying from somewhere they couldn't see.

Looks up as if making the attempt and failing.

ABEL:

Who said Indians?

RUTH:

Well, then, robbers. Look!
I'd be a hundred birds, with terrible claws
Pecking, pecking at them out of the sky.

Imitates the action with great vigor, laughing.

ABEL:

Who said robbers? Anyway, there's only
One, and he's no robber. You know who.

RUTH:

Sh-h. Don't name him. That might bring him—quick.

ABEL:

Resuming with the rake.

You stop right there now! Turn around and git!

DINAH:

Without looking at him.

No, Abel, no.

*Both children give her all of their attention, as to one who
rarely speaks. RUTH stands up and touches her cheek and*

mouth; ABEL *lets the heavy end of the rake drop to the floor with a thud.*

> Be nice. Be gentle. Wait.

All three are silent as JEREMIAH *comes in at the lower left corner of the stage, carrying a small basket—which he drops in amazement when he sees them.*

JEREMIAH:

Dinah, my dear girl! And Ruth! Abel,
I'm not surprised *you're* here, but—now, what's this?
Was no one home there?

RUTH:

> We came back.

JEREMIAH:

> I see.

My eyes are not as bad as my old bones.
Blinks.
Dinah, did I hear you saying something?
That's rare enough. Say it again, for me.
But she has relapsed into her habitual trance.
Ruth—Abel—has a cat got both your tongues?
Was no one there—that it? Or if they were,
Did Nathan Hard do tricks? Abel, my boy——

ABEL:

He's coming over here.

JEREMIAH:

> Who is?

ABEL:

> You know,

The man you mentioned.

JEREMIAH:

> Ha! He has no name.

Suddenly excited.

But what is this? That's good! That's very good!
Nathan has cracked his shell. I wouldn't have thought—
Yet wait a minute! Why didn't the girls stay?
What happened over there? Abel, you gosling——

RUTH:
He's coming sure, great-grandpa.

JEREMIAH:
                      Great wildcats!
Great hummingbirds, great ravens in the wind!
But why?—and why?

Waits; then, when they say nothing—the children only steal-
ing glances at each other—he picks up his basket and pokes
among its contents.

             Well, so it goes. I ask
Too much and get too little. But I'm glad
He's coming to repay our family call.
Maybe he missed *me*. Ha! did he now?

The children shake their heads.

He might have wondered. But if things went well,
No matter.

Pokes into his basket again.

          I put in the afternoon
Picking fall posies; they're the best of the year,
To my old way of thinking, and to hers
You never saw. Why, even Dinah there—
You don't remember your Grandmother Horn,
Do you? No, she died—oh, dear, so long
Ago I can't be sure of how she looked.
Yes, I can, too, when she walked in asters
As I did today, and stooped and picked
An armful just the color of her eyes.
There's many shades of asters, but all blue:
Some light, some dark. Well, she was in between.
The gentians do her justice, the fringed ones,
That both conceal their beauty and confess it—

But shyly. I've been told I shouldn't pick them,
And most days I don't; but by the sawmill
They crowded so together, I was bold
And took one each for all of us. Here, Ruth—
It's like you too, and like your mother—there,
Give Dinah that one. Abel, you're a boy,
But don't look down on flowers; they look up
To you, remember that. Now here at the bottom—
See? Grass of Parnassus: solitary
Stars, so small, so white, with delicate
Dark veins, like pencil lines on ivory.
I should have brought something for Nathan, too,
To celebrate. He's coming—that is good,
Ah, very good—to sit with us and talk
As in the old days he did. Yet he was busy,
And never stayed long. But I remember——

> REBECCA *comes through the door with a light shawl which
> she throws over* DINAH's *shoulders.*

Becky, you remember, as these don't,
How restless Nathan was: eyes on his watch,
Considering; then getting up and going,
Sometimes without a single word. But still
He came. And now—Becky, have you heard?—
He's coming once again. That's very good!

> REBECCA:

For the moment ignoring him.

Dinah, you must go in with the children.

> DINAH *leans back more firmly in her chair.*

It will be chilly soon, with the sun down,
And you are tired—I know it. Then, child,
This isn't the place for you. Not now. It's dangerous.
You understand? It's dangerous. Come in
With Grandma. Abel, Ruth, you help her, won't you?

> *All three of them remain where they were, looking over the
> audience at something they imagine there.*

JEREMIAH:

Drumming the side of the basket with his hand.

You hear her, don't you? In with you!

RUTH *and* ABEL *start, reluctantly, then glance at each other and stop.*

RUTH:

Abel, if it was Indians——

JEREMIAH:

If it were.

Indians? Indians? Ha! so simple then.

RUTH:

If it was robbers, Abel——

JEREMIAH:

simpler still——

RUTH:

Remember, birds and arrows.

Swings her arms wildly.

But the rake

Might be some help at first.

Imitates him, fiercely.

Now go, now git!

JEREMIAH:

Do as she told you, then—go, git! Besides,
I've got a thing or two to talk about,
And I don't want you with us—her and me.
Becky, you can guess. Stay here a minute.
They know the way.

REBECCA, *who has taken* DINAH'*s hand to lead her in, hesitates, then puts it in* RUTH'*s hand, who guides* DINAH *through the door,* ABEL *following, his head rebelliously turned sidewise toward the rake. As they leave,* AMOS *ap-*

pears at the lower left corner of the stage where JEREMIAH *had entered. He is pale and serious, watching and listening intently.*

Now, Becky! What's all this?
Ruth wouldn't say—or couldn't.

REBECCA:

Oh, she couldn't.
She doesn't understand. You want to know
Why Dinah's back. Well, Josephine has told me.
They're all in there—Josephine, she told me.

JEREMIAH:

In God's name, what?

REBECCA:

Don't swear. It's serious, Jerry.
Sighs deeply; cannot go on, then does.
I don't know how to say it. Dinah sang,
And Nathan, he——

JEREMIAH:

He what!

REBECCA:

—is coming here
To murder Peter.
AMOS *gives a start, but does not betray his presence.*

JEREMIAH:
Sets the basket down slowly at his feet.
Murder! Nathan's mad.

REBECCA:
No wonder, maybe. Dinah sang a song——

JEREMIAH:
Oh, that.

REBECCA:

But there was more. They couldn't stop her.
A song about who Ruth's father was—
Oh, Jerry, it was David! Think of it! David!

JEREMIAH:

I've thought of it. I knew. I've always known.
I learned of it when Peter did—he knows.

REBECCA:

Groans.

You never told. Jerry, that was wrong.

JEREMIAH:

Was it? How tell Nathan such a thing?

REBECCA:

Better then than now. But did you know
The worst thing of all? How David died?

JEREMIAH:

Why, everyone knows that.

REBECCA:

Well, then you don't.
Listen, Jerry. Peter murdered him.
AMOS *nods solemnly; folds his hands.*

JEREMIAH:

Oh, no!
Staggers to the edge of the porch and sits there staring at her.

REBECCA:

Oh, yes! He rolled the stone, and Dinah
Saw it. That's what took her wits away.
She saw it; and it's still the only thing,
I guess, the poor girl sees. It goes on falling
Inside of her. I comprehend more now
Than ever I hoped to; more than I have heart to.

NEVER, NEVER ASK HIS NAME

The song told Nathan all of this; and so
He drove them out of house; said he was coming
To find Peter alone——

JEREMIAH:

He won't do that.

REBECCA:

Perhaps the children thought so.

JEREMIAH:

Yes, I see.

Where's Peter now?

REBECCA:

In there. But by himself,
In Patience's old room. He says for us
To go to some safe place. He isn't hiding.
He'll come out when he needs to—so he said.
He won't have us shielding him—not Jack,
Nor anybody younger than he is.

JEREMIAH:

I'm older.

REBECCA:

You stay out. He said that plainly.

JEREMIAH:

He did? My God of Gods, to think that Peter——

REBECCA:

Don't swear.

JEREMIAH:

Don't you be silly. Peter, Peter!
It can't be true.

REBECCA:

Ah, but it's too true.
Don't waste your breath refusing to believe it.

JEREMIAH:

And if I did, what would I understand?
Why, everything, as you do with Dinah.
Oh, but I'd rather not.

REBECCA:

So I, with Dinah.

JEREMIAH:

I see, I see.

Lost in thought.

But when is Nathan coming?

REBECCA:

He said this afternoon.

JEREMIAH:

Looking intently at the house.

Patience's old room.

Can't I go up there?

REBECCA:

Looking where he does, so that neither of them sees NATHAN,
*who, gun in hand, quietly appears at the side of the stage
opposite to where* JEREMIAH *had come in, and where* AMOS
is. He is unaware of AMOS; *but* AMOS, *seeing him arrive,
starts over as if to speak to him, then waits. Meanwhile*
NATHAN *stands without a motion or a sound.*

No. Leave Peter alone.

He wants it that way.

JOSEPHINE *enters through the door and motions to them both
without being aware of* NATHAN *or of* AMOS.

Josephine, I'm coming.

JOSEPHINE:

You both are, and please be quick about it.
The youngest ones are in, so now the oldest—
You come too, lest there be waste of life.
No telling——

Turns slightly, sees NATHAN, *and screams at the top of her voice. The old people, following her eyes, groan as one person. A moment of utter silence succeeds the scream, with none of them moving.*

> Jack! Jack!

JACK:

Comes running through the door.

> What is it, Jophy?

JOSEPHINE:

Look!

JACK halts for a second, then comes forward to stand in front of JOSEPHINE, *who continues behind him.*

> He's here! He meant it!

NATHAN:

Quietly at first.

> Didn't you think——

JOSEPHINE:

I didn't think at all. I only ran
When the rest did, because you cracked your whip.
It didn't seem to me I heard much more
Than that. And maybe I never did. You still
Can't mean it.

NATHAN:

> No? Where's Peter? Is he gone?
I gave him time to go—to think he was free.
But he's not free. I'll follow him as far
As a coward's feet can carry him.

JACK:

> He's free.
He's not afraid. She is—

Jerking his head to indicate JOSEPHINE.

> and those—

Again, to indicate REBECCA *and* JEREMIAH.

> —but not

My father, Mr. Hard.

JEREMIAH:

> Who says *I* am?

Nathan, Nathan, throw that thing away
And talk to us—to me.

NATHAN:

> A waste of words.

Old man Horn, you've wasted thousands of them.
Why, you've done nothing else. What makes you think——

JEREMIAH:

Only just now I learned it. How can it be?
That's it—how can it? Terrible. Ten years,
And no one knew but Dinah.

NATHAN:

> You'd have liked

To know yourself—is that it, Mr. Horn?
What then?

JEREMIAH:

> Why, I'd have told you. The worst thing

Was that *you* didn't know, and so blasphemed
The Maker of this world—His winds, His waters,
His animals and flowers.

> *Caresses his basket.* AMOS *lowers his eyes to the ground.*

> You put your curse

On innocence and guilt together; darkened
The whole sky, for children and for men;
For us as well as you. A waste of woe,
With no sharp anger cleansing it, as lightning
Does, as thunder—crack! and all impurities
Are burned away. If I had told you then—
Ah, and added why——

NATHAN:

Be still, old man!

JEREMIAH:

Not yet I won't, not yet—if you had known
All of the worst at once——

NATHAN:

Then what? Then what?

JEREMIAH:

I cannot say for sure. I'm not a prophet
Backward. But it might have been over soon;
Not hanging, as it has been, not decaying
In dampness, darkness.

REBECCA:
Stirring.

Jerry, that's enough,
You can't go on forever. And don't you notice?
It makes no difference to him what you say.
Peter!

For she has seen him slowly emerge out of the shadows in the doorway. JOSEPHINE, *gasping, whirls about and faces him;* JACK, *turning more slowly, looks at him over* JOSEPHINE's *shoulder; and* JEREMIAH, *dropping the basket, raises both of his hands, palms forward, half in warning, half in blessing.* NATHAN *does not lift his gun.* AMOS *does not move.*

Don't come out here! Jack, stand there
As long as he does—Josephine, not you!

For JOSEPHINE *has shifted to a position that makes her an additional shield against* NATHAN.

See to the children. Peter, let her pass.

PETER:
Surprisingly calm.

That's right, the children. When I heard you scream,
Jophy, the first thing I thought about

Was them. They're in the parlor, and both doors
Are locked. Dinah's with them. Here's the key—
Go in and keep them quiet. You can pass.

> *She does not move.*

And Jack, go with her. I don't need you here,
Either of you. Mother—and Father Horn—
And Amos, for I spy you there—

> *All turn, astonished, and see* AMOS, *who keeps his eyes on*
> PETER. NATHAN *glances at him briefly, as at an unwelcome in-*
> *truder, then returns his gaze to* PETER.

                                        Amos,
It isn't what you thought; it's more, it's worse;
It's me.

AMOS:

        Yes, Peter, I know. I guessed,
And now I know.

PETER:

> *His shoulders suddenly sagging.*

                        I wondered. But my good friend,
My counsellor of old, please leave this thing
Just as you find it. Just as you see me now—
Well, that is how I *would* be. No man's help,
Not even yours, is needed.

NATHAN:

                                Go on home,
Parson. This is no sore you can poultice.
Your God is not concerned—He never was—
With men like him and me—with stones——

> *His voice breaks as* AMOS *does not reply.*

PETER:

Amos, it is too late. The thing was done
Too long ago for even your great God——

NATHAN:

Great God!

PETER:

And so I say to all that hear me——

JEREMIAH:

No, Peter, we'll stay with you.
Drops his hands.

AMOS:

So will I.

With Nathan, too.
NATHAN *shrugs contemptuously.*

With all of you.

PETER:

Jack,

Do as I say, regardless of that good man.
Jophy, too—all of you—leave me alone
With Nathan. That's the way I want it now.
Look. He's waiting.

They all turn involuntarily and see NATHAN'*s hands restless
on the gun, which he lifts from the ground, then sets down
again.*

Leave my friend to me.

JACK:

Your friend! He isn't ours!

JOSEPHINE:

Forget that now.

Here's something worse.

REBECCA:

Peter, we are staying.

And Jophy, Jack, don't move—I tell you, don't.
I wasn't there to hear him, but I know

He meant it. I can see with my own eyes.
I feel it in him, too. Yes, I'm afraid.
Oh, why don't neighbors come—Mrs. Johansen
Senior, or that simpleton of George's—
Who would laugh at him now? I never did,
But now! Oh, anything to break the spell!
Nathan, at least say something.

NATHAN:

                          I can wait
Like this, without a word, as long as he can.

REBECCA:

But Peter spoke—you heard him.

NATHAN:

                          I can wait
Till one of them steps away. Both will, in time—
It's not in nature to stand there like that—
And then——

JEREMIAH:

                In nature, Nathan! Wilderness,
You mean. You've made God's world a wilderness,
With nothing in it but the ghost of David—

NATHAN:

Devilish old man! Must I kill *you*
To stop your mouth? I didn't come for that,
But have a care; you'll say one word too many.

JEREMIAH:

I'll say all I have got. And mind you, Nathan,
I'm not for murder—David's either.

REBECCA:

                         Hush!
Nobody else can say that name.

NATHAN:

No, only

Peter. I am waiting till he says it:
"I killed David." Then I'll know.

JACK:

You know

Already.

NATHAN:

Simpleton! Like her—a song!

JACK:

Oh, no, I mean he said it plain this morning.
"I did it." We all heard.

NATHAN:

He had to then.

But now once more he has to. I must hear it
In his own doorway, where I came to find him.

AMOS:

You'd kill a man confessing?

NATHAN:

Would, and will.

Confessing? Merely saying what he must,
So you, so these can hear it. And myself.

PETER:

Motioning to JOSEPHINE *and* JACK.

Stand away, you two. I want no such
Advantage over Nathan.

JACK:

He has one.

It's in his hands.

PETER:

And I could have equalled it,
But didn't. That was my own choice, children.
Do as I say. Give Nathan his advantage.

NATHAN:

Noble! Do you think this will disarm me?

PETER:

Nothing will, I know. You have the power,
To use or not to use, that I had once.
I used it, but in secret—so I thought.
You have these witnesses, and still you say
You'll use what you have there. I must admire
This colder strength than I had then. Children,
Respect it. Stand away.

They do not stir.

For I had then
No strength at all. Only the rock was strong,
That heard, I thought, what I heard—David saying
No, and No, to Dinah. And his reason
Was that he feared his father.

NATHAN:

None of that!

Raises the gun, though not to his shoulder.

I've waited long enough. Now I must cut
Clean through. Three—one—what difference is there?

PETER:

This difference—look!

Suddenly reaches forward and with all his force sweeps
JOSEPHINE *to the left,* JACK *to the right.*

Now you have only me.
And all you need's the strength—the cold strength—

REBECCA:

In a terrible whisper as NATHAN, *deliberately, takes aim.* AMOS *starts forward as if to interfere, restrains himself with visible effort, and stops.*

Peter! My only boy!

PETER:

Mother, be still.

He is unaware, as the others are, that ELIZABETH, *out of breath from running, has appeared behind* AMOS, *whom she pushes aside without knowing or caring who he is. Startled, he lets her pass him, and looks over her shoulder as she cries out. The moment she does so, he lifts a hand to bless her, but does not touch even her dress.*

ELIZABETH:

Nathan!

REBECCA, *turning, starts toward her, stumbles, and falls at her feet.* JEREMIAH, *for whom stooping is difficult, nevertheless lowers himself to* REBECCA's *side, stroking her head as he looks up at* ELIZABETH. *The rest remain as they were, their eyes fixed on* NATHAN, *who slowly, as if the sound of* ELIZABETH's *scream had taken a long time to reach him, lowers the gun again, though he does not look her way.* PETER *continues to face him.*

Thank God, thank God I still could speak!
I prayed to Him not to take all my breath.
You heard me, Nathan. Oh, dear God, he heard me!

Nearly collapsing, staggers to a pillar of the porch and holds herself with difficulty upright.

All of you, thank God!

As REBECCA *raises her head, and* JEREMIAH *stands up,* JOSEPHINE *and* JACK *start toward her; but stop, frozen, when they hear* NATHAN.

NATHAN:

        Stay where you are.
This isn't over yet. And Parson Gold,
That means you too.

  ELIZABETH, *turning and seeing* AMOS *behind her, totters toward him, her hands out; then recovers her strength and turns again to* NATHAN.

       No matter how you snivel
And pray, and hope the end is nice and quiet,
This isn't over yet.

ELIZABETH:

        No, not till I say
One thing—two things. Nathan, you love the truth.
Then listen to it. Oh, I know it now.

  AMOS *leans closer, not to miss her words.*

NATHAN:

Remarkable!

ELIZABETH:

      Please listen. David's the one
You're angry at. He always was. He tried
Over and over to please you, and he failed.
Your faith in him—so terrible—
Was not in him at all, but in the dream
You dreamed and never woke from; never till now.

  NATHAN *turns his head halfway, as if listening against his will.*

When he deceived you—

  He turns the whole way, frowning.

      —Oh, he had to, Nathan—
It was to save *that.* You never knew—
Nor I—of him and Dinah. Who can measure
The panic in his mind when this bore fruit
That nothing would be able to conceal.
Oh, which was worse: the death David died,

Or the one you would have died in months to come?
But darling, Peter saved you.

NATHAN:

Groans.

                                    Lizzie, Lizzie!

ELIZABETH:

Listen to the truth. You say you love it.

NATHAN:

As if you knew.

ELIZABETH:

                    I know that Peter gave you
Grief—pure grief—instead of rage so great
You might have wished your own son were dead.

NATHAN *groans again and closes his eyes.*

Dinah saved you, too, until today;
And saved her father. Now we all are naked.
The song stripped us. You no longer hate
God's world but one man in it, whose quick death
Would quiet nothing; yet you came to kill him.
But there was someone else you came to kill.

NATHAN:

Who?

ELIZABETH:

    David.

NATHAN:

Almost screams.
                    David!

ELIZABETH:

                    Yes. Which iron
Went deeper in this morning? There were two
In that soft song. Which of them found your heart?

And if one did—why, the heart is where
Forgiveness never dies.

NATHAN:
Hoarsely.

                              I can't forgive him.

ELIZABETH:
Who?

NATHAN:
    How can you ask it?

ELIZABETH:
                              But I do.
I ask you to forgive our own sweet son—

NATHAN:
David!—

ELIZABETH:
        Who died despairing of it. Listen,
Nathan. It never is too late. Be such
A father as God is, forgiving the whole
World for being eternally what it is:
A place of error—none of us knows how much.
If you can find it in you to forgive
David, all of the rest will follow sometime.
Dinah forgave him——

PETER:
                        And I did, that very
Day—oh, if I could have said it then,
With all of you listening, after the lamentation
Ceased. The silence then! If I could have broken it—

JEREMIAH:
Lifting REBECCA *to her feet.*
You should have. It is always best to speak.

REBECCA:

Or else, Jerry, not to. Leave the poor souls
Alone.

NATHAN:

Laughing all at once, hysterically.

Old man, old man, you have the secret.
Let the tongue wag—that's it. Let every soul
Say everything. Let language be the lord
Of life. Of death, too. Oh, my God,
I am to say that I forgive my son,
Believing he will hear. If he has ears,
He'll heed me—is that it? There is no darkness
Anywhere—no, no, no, no, no, no.

Exhausted, pauses, while the others stand appalled. ELIZA-
BETH, *however, looks both fearful and elated.*

They say I made a darkness——

PETER:

No, I did.

If, looking down on David, I could have said:
"I killed him, then I instantly forgave him
The thing I killed him for, I love the boy,
I killed him but I love him"; and if Dinah,
Cursing me, had told; and Nathan had come
Like tigers at my throat—all natural,
All proper to the horror of that time—
And Father Horn, if you had said your say—
For you knew something Nathan should have known——

JEREMIAH:

I meant all this. Silence is fool's gold,
And I too was a fool, I helped to build
The darkness.

NATHAN:

Darkness! And shall there now be light?
Shall we all cry together?

*The gun trembles in his hands as he turns to them one after
the other, shouting, however, only to himself.*

Would the sound
Of that be like a lamp somebody lit?

Removes one hand from the gun and draws it across his eyes.

Lizzie, I heard you. All of you that spoke,
I heard you. Even the Reverend, the still one—
I heard him thinking those sly thoughts of his
That slipped among us—oh, so very sly—
To change me.

Lowers his voice a little; speaks slowly and clearly.

And they did. You all did. Lizzie,
You did, first of all.

She takes a step toward him; stops.

So I'm to forgive
My boy. Well then, I do.

Trancelike, to the audience.

David, David,
Hear me! I forgive you as your mother
Told me to. And Dinah.

Closes his eyes.

Then if those——

ELIZABETH:

Breathlessly.

Nathan! You came here—must you still——

NATHAN:

No.
Not while that man is there behind you—no,
Not while he looks and listens.

Bitter again.

God, God,
Why did he come?

Pauses.

                          Yet, Lizzie, he did come,
And so did you. I'm glad of it—I'm glad.

Grips the gun; waits; then walks to AMOS *and lays it in his
hands.*

REBECCA:

Sinks to her knees as AMOS *does.*

Thank God!

AMOS:

            I'll take this in. There will be dew,
And that is bad for weapons.

NATHAN:

                    Let it be.

PETER:

Advancing to the front of the porch, unsteadily.

                              Don't leave us,
Nathan.

Waits.

        There is more for me to say
Than I know how to.

NATHAN *shrugs away the need of words.*

                Please, though, let me try.

Pauses.

Thank you for my life. If it *is* mine,
Not David's. Or else—

Goes on with difficulty.

                    the law's.

All except NATHAN *stop moving and stand silent;* NATHAN
*starts to make a gesture of impatience, which is arrested sud-
denly by* AMOS'S *voice, louder and stronger than before.*

AMOS:

                                        Yes. The law's.
Your life, Peter, has never been your own
Since you took David's.

PETER:

His hands over his face.

                              Oh, I know, I know!
Ten years I've been a dead man.

JOSEPHINE:

                                    No, you haven't.
You have been good to us. We love you, Father.
You gave me Jack and Abel. What would I be
Without those two? You have been kind as sun
On gardens, and we blossomed—why, to please *you!*

PETER:

And so you did. You pleased me—all of my young ones
Pleased me.

JOSEPHINE:

                    Think of Dinah, whom your very
Voice was music to. I've seen her smile
When a far door opened; she knew your step.

PETER:

Trembling.

But Dinah! Nathan, you were right. I changed
My daughter, I destroyed her. Had I spoken,
And the whole world been witness, who is to say
She wouldn't have suffered only as all of us suffer
When time brings on its changes? But my silence
Fathered her own, and festered in that brain
I loved so when she used it to beguile me,
As a bright child, with songs.

Shudders.

                                        But not *that* song!

AMOS:

Which Nathan heard, I know. So then he learned——

NATHAN:

Your bill of particulars is long enough.
Please leave my own name out of it. Don't preach
With me for text.

PETER:

               He isn't preaching, Nathan,
Unless the truth's a sermon. Yes, you too.
I blasted *your* ten years. A natural grief—
Forgive me—grew to something so unearthly,
Nobody comprehended. The root of it
Was ignorance of what I did; or was.

REBECCA:

You were Peter. You still are.

PETER:

                     And have
No further license, Mother, to be at all.

REBECCA:

Covers her face.

Oh, oh!

JOSEPHINE:

Hurrying toward PETER.

         Don't be stubborn. It was long
Ago, and you have suffered, as *you* say.
That makes a world of difference—doesn't it?

Looks wildly at the others.

JACK:

She's right.

PETER:

Unaffected.

The life that I thank Nathan for
Was not my life. So, Amos, what must I do?

AMOS:

Tell everything to all the world. But first,
To what you call the law—and so do I,
But there is one above it that I credit
With a more perfect knowledge. God is just,
And punishes. And so most men are just,
And punish. But the mercy in His mind
Sheds down on ours as well; and so I hope——

NATHAN:

You hope the sheriff turns his back on this—
Spits, and swears he never heard a word.

AMOS:

Then he is not a man. I think he is one;
I say he will be serious. How the powers
Beyond him will dispose I have no inkling.
But they must hear it all. Peter confessed
To you and these. Now it must be to those;
And all my hope is, they are men of God.

NATHAN:

You know they aren't. Tomkins—Underwood——

AMOS:

I know that they are like ourselves, being men;
And being men, images of Him
That made them.

PETER:

                    As I was, until I broke
The mold. But Amos—when?

AMOS:

Shifts his feet.

                              The time is now.

PETER:

Looking at REBECCA, *who keeps her hands over her face.*
This moment?

AMOS:

        Yes.

NATHAN:

         Mules! But I'll go with you.

JACK:

So will I.

Moves to PETER's *side.*

NATHAN:

      Hold your horses! Amos,
You can't lead Peter off like this.

ELIZABETH:

               Oh, Nathan,
Bless you. This is more than I can bear.
You want to save him when you came to—dearest,
Why should I cry at what delights me so?
It changes all my blood to warm again.

Pauses.

And yet—and yet—

Wrings her hands.

            Peter is saving himself
Without your help or anyone's.

Covers her face.

              It's best.

PETER:

Listen, Nathan. Amos and I alone——

NATHAN:

That's nonsense.

PETER:

                    Possibly. But when I go
I want no champion near, no one to plead
Or mitigate. I shall not plead. I'll tell
Our story, and let it end as time decides.
We cannot end it; we have not the wisdom.

NATHAN:
Who has?

PETER:

          I only know, not you, not me,
Not Amos, even.

AMOS:

                    Myself the least of all.

NATHAN:
Don't whinny.

ELIZABETH:
Recovering.
                    Nathan!

NATHAN:

                    I distrust humility
Whenever it sounds like meekness. Meekness I hate—
You know that, Lizzie.

ELIZABETH:

                    But think of what they're doing!
When shall we see Peter again? Think, Nathan!

NATHAN:
Why——

PETER:

          Possibly not ever.
All gasp. REBECCA, *who had risen, sinks to her knees again.*
                    At least

I'm going as though—
Hesitates.

for good.

JACK:
Stamping his feet.

Damn! Damn!

JOSEPHINE:
Be still, Jack, be still.

JEREMIAH:

It's good to go,
Peter. But keep the hope we all must have.

PETER:
Starting down the steps toward AMOS.

I will not nurse it. Nathan, I thought to speak
Of many things with you. Consider we did.
And understand I am at last——

NATHAN:

Not happy,
Don't say happy.

PETER:

Only free.

NATHAN:

Only
Senseless.

ELIZABETH:

Nathan, Nathan!

NATHAN:

For a man
To put his neck into a noose——

JOSEPHINE:
Screams so that JACK *runs to her helplessly.*
                                        Oh, no!
Don't say it! Mercy on us, one and all.

AMOS:
Starting off with PETER.
So be it. Goodnight, friends.
    Turns from one to another.
                            Goodnight. Goodnight.

NATHAN:
More quietly, to PETER's *back.*
Then you are not to be changed. If it is madness—
Superfluous, unprofitable madness—
So be it, I say too. Peter, goodnight!
    Hurries to him, stops him, shakes his hand.

ELIZABETH:
Clasping her hands.
Nathan, you understand at last. His soul——

NATHAN:
Let us not speak of it; not now; not yet.

ELIZABETH:
Nodding.
Leave it in peace. But Nathan! You understood!

PETER:
Glancing up at the house.
Goodnight to all our children.

JEREMIAH:
                            Living—dead——

ELIZABETH:
Oh, all of them are living, all at last
Are loved in light, not darkness. Day already

Breaks on two we never knew we had:
A daughter, a granddaughter.

NATHAN *nods, gravely.*

JACK:

Why, she's right!
Whoever thought of that?

REBECCA:

I did.

JEREMIAH:

I did,
I do, and I rejoice. The generations——

JOSEPHINE:

As a distant whistle blows.
Listen. That was Adam. They'll be coming
Hungry from the Fair. Adam blows
That thing so hard, you'd think his brains would burst.

JACK:

It's a new one, maybe.

JOSEPHINE:

No, the old.
Controlling herself at last.
Goodnight, father.

PETER:

Goodnight, dear. Be calm—

JOSEPHINE:

Oh, yes! Oh, yes!

JACK:

She will be if she can.
Helplessly.
Goodnight, father.

PETER:

Goodnight, Jack. Help her—

REBECCA:

Oh, oh!

PETER:

And *her*. Remember, Mother——

REBECCA:

Faintly.

What?

PETER:

Why, everything. Leave nothing out.

REBECCA:

Moans.

I'll do my best.

PETER:

That's good. I love you, Mother.
A moment of complete silence ensues.

ELIZABETH:

Nathan,
As he beckons for her to go.
    wait for me.
Runs after PETER *and kisses him.*
              Goodnight, old friend.

PETER:

Takes her hand, then turns once more and looks up at the house.

Listen!
The organ is heard offstage, playing familiar music as a familiar voice sings unfamiliar words.

DINAH:

My Savior sings, and I give heed.
 What does he sing, my Savior?
I would I were as wise as he,
 But my own words come lamely.

I would I might tell all the world
 How sweet he is, my Savior;
How honey lies upon his lips,
 As if he were King David.

He sings to me, and I rejoice.
 Because I know his meaning.
But never, never ask his name.
 Good evening, sirs, good evening.

All stand motionless till the song is ended. Then PETER *and* AMOS *disappear together;* JEREMIAH *helps* REBECCA *to her feet and starts leading her away; and the rest go off severally, but not before a whistle is heard again, louder than the first time, and children's voices rise shrilly above the sound of carriage wheels and horses' feet.*

Curtain.

A LITTLE
NIGHT MUSIC

_____

A Comedy in Three Acts

•

LIST OF PERSONS
In the Order of Their Appearance

AMY GODOLPHIN
ADAM MONTAGUE
FRANCIS BIRDLOVE
FELIX WRY
MONA HOWE
JASON HOWE
DR. GAIL HORSMAN
HELEN PARISH

Scene

New York: A Room in the House of JASON HOWE.

Time

The Present.

Act One

The central room of JASON HOWE'S *house, an hour after dinner. Doors left and right. A hi-fi set in the far right corner.*

A dance tune is playing as the curtain rises. ADAM *and* AMY *continue dancing; they look into each other's eyes, smiling as they meet and part; then whirl away, separate, around the room; then meet again in the center, laughing without sound. After a minute or two the record stops, and* ADAM *runs over to start it once more.* AMY, *following him with her eyes, snaps her fingers and skips to join him. She places her hand over his and shakes her head.*

AMY:

Darling, no more of other people's music.
Let's make our own.

Stamps her feet and whirls lightly a number of times; returns to him, pretends to be dizzy, and lets him catch her with his arm about her waist.

ADAM:

Kissing her.

       As if we could.

AMY:

Stands free again.

> We can!

Listen to these words. I made them up
While that was going.

Points to the record.

> Listen to me, Adam,

And say them with me after.

*Starts to improvise a step; changes it; experiments some more;
seems satisfied.*

> Listen good;

Half speaks, half sings; retreats, advances, while ADAM, *falling
in with her, moves as she moves.*

You come to me,
I go to you;
Then back, then back;
Now come again;
Right hand, left hand,
Both so true,
Both so true,
Forever when.

Suddenly breaks away.

There! How's that?

ADAM:

Has not stopped shuffling his feet.

> Fine! *You* listen, Amy.

*Repeats the song as she returns to him and dances with him
to the end.*

But isn't there more? We could go on with this.

Unseen by either of them, FRANCIS *and* FELIX *have come in
and now stand watching them.*

AMY:

Well, then, there *is* more. Only this much, though.

They dance again, more and more wildly, as she sings.

Ah, my sweet,
My perfect one,
Each is each
When all is done.
So round and round—
Run!—run!—
Which is the moon?
Which is the sun?

Suddenly sees FRANCIS *and* FELIX; *is breathless.*

But Adam! There's an audience!

ADAM:

Not too pleased.

Hello.

FRANCIS:

You didn't need an audience, my dears.
Yet here we are, and it was ravishing.
Thank you for—

Hesitates.

ADAM:

What?

FRANCIS:

For being young, and being—
Or so I think—absolutely in love.
A new thing in this old world.

FELIX:

Sardonically.

The oldest
Thing of all. Don't be an ass, Birdlove.
The new thing would be for such as these
Not to. They can't help it. Or *he* can't.

Points moodily at ADAM.

AMY:

Or me, Felix. Why do you leave me out?
What have I left undone? Shall I begin,
Here and now, to eat him up?

> *Crosses and kisses* ADAM.

                          Face first?

FRANCIS:

Don't do that.

FELIX:

                Why not? She had devoured
The cheeks and eyes before we came; the rest
Can follow if she has the stomach for it.

AMY:

> *Aware that* ADAM *resents this.*

Oh, Felix!

> *Turns away from him.*

                Francis, you're the nice one tonight.
But then you always are—Felix only
Sometimes.

ADAM:

> *With sarcasm.*

                Sometimes? Not lately, though.

AMY:

Sh-h-h.

> *Puts her hands out to him.*

                Sweetheart, shall we dance again?

ADAM:

> *Turning his back to all of them.*

No.

FRANCIS:
Now that's a pity.

FELIX:

What's a pity?
He doesn't like us looking on; that's all.
And I for one could miss it without pain.
Come on, Francis. We'll find the others somewhere.
I thought they would be here.

AMY:

The library——

FELIX:
Ah! Where no one ever reads.

AMY:

I do.

FELIX:
Little Women.

AMY:

Guess again.

FELIX:
Grimaces.

I can't.
I'm barren of conjecture. Plutarch? Shakespeare?

AMY:
Thank you, no.

FELIX:

Spinoza? Dr. Freud?

AMY:
Laughing.
Thank you, thank you. It will be my secret.

FELIX:

Keep it, then. And keep yourself, my dear.
Francis, let us leave them to their vices,
Such as they are. Come on.

Goes out with FRANCIS.

ADAM:

Echoing FELIX.

"My dear." Sweetheart,
Watch that man.

AMY:

What do you mean?

ADAM:

"My dear"—
What right has he to—

AMY:

Mimicking him.

Right? Why, what a word!
He's almost Uncle Felix to me—has been
As long as I remember.

ADAM:

Yes, I know.
Uncle Francis, too.

AMY:

He said "my dears."

ADAM:

To both of us.

AMY:

Well—

Goes to him.

Adam, what's the matter?

ADAM:

I don't like the way he looks at you,
Or talks to you, or thinks of you—God knows
What the man thinks: I like that least of all.

AMY:

Shocked.

The man! As if he were a stranger to us.
He's Uncle Jason's oldest friend almost,
Unless Francis is. Aunt Mona's, too.
The four of them are what I first remember;
And all of them so kind. Why not "my dear"?
I *am* dear to him; or hope I am.

ADAM:

Too dear these days.

AMY:

Puzzled.

You mean he's different now?

ADAM:

Lately, yes. And you're so nice to him,
It makes me sick.

AMY:

Turns away; her voice trembles.

I'm nice to everybody.
An orphan has to be.

ADAM:

Me included.

AMY:

Turns back to him.

Adam! We were dancing as one person,
And now you make us two. Adam, Adam,
I love you—don't you know?

ADAM:

Takes her into his arms.

How could I not?
Yes, yes! And I love you—do you believe me?

AMY:

Nods.

But then you say these things. Uncle Jason—
Think of him. He never has been jealous
Of Felix—not one minute—or of Francis.

ADAM:

Felix! Francis!

AMY:

Don't you know?

ADAM:

Know what?
I only know they're here, come sunset, like two
Evening stars. All day, too, if they can.
Even if they don't live here, this is home.
I wonder if they really have addresses.

AMY:

Smiles; nods; then is serious.

Both of them are hopelessly in love
With my Aunt Mona—oh, so hopelessly,
It isn't funny any more; or tragic, either.
I think I knew it when I was a child,
Just brought here when my mother and father died.
And yet I couldn't have known it then; though soon
I did—I've always known it—I've lived with it.
And so has Uncle Jason. *He's* not jealous.

ADAM:

Of old friends? His, too. It can't be what
You think.

AMY:

   It is, it is. But there's the wonder.
All four of them are friends, back to the bare
Beginning of the world. And Uncle Jason
Lives with it like God, who never minds
How many love how many. And why should He?
He made the world with love, and so *for* love.

ADAM:

A matchmaker?

AMY:

     No. But He's not jealous.

ADAM:

They say He is.

AMY:

     Of evil, not of good.
Of hatred, and of jealousy in us.

ADAM:

Kissing her.

I stand corrected.

AMY:

*Pulling away as voices are heard, some of them angry, out-
side the room.*
     Listen! Here they come.
All of us, remember now, are friends—
Old friends. So very nice. Old
Friends—remember, Adam. So let's be.

ADAM:

I never said we weren't.

Kisses her quickly.

AMY:

     Sh-h-h. I hear
The doctor, too. That's good.

A half-open door swings open to its full width and MONA
HOWE *comes in, talking excitedly. She is followed at once
by* FELIX *and* FRANCIS, *then by* JASON HOWE; DR. HORSMAN,
after an interval, brings up the rear.

MONA:

Felix, I mean it.
Leave that girl alone. She's mine—she's ours—

Jerks her heard toward JASON.

But certainly not yours. Leave Amy alone.

JASON *gestures to remind her that* AMY *is present.*

Oh, I don't care if she hears this. It's time
She did. Amy—

Cannot go on, seeing that AMY *is shocked and speechless, as*
ADAM *is.*

FELIX:

Disconcerted—an unusual state for him.
Mona! Please!

MONA:

Be still.
Can silliness be silent? Then be silent.
I know you have no gift for it, but try.
At your age, to moon over a maiden—

DOCTOR:

Alert as if after long indifference.
Maiden? Who's a maiden? Technical.

MONA:

Physician, don't be foul.

DOCTOR:

Looking at her over his glasses.

Occupational.

ADAM:

Mrs. Howe, it happens that we two
    Takes AMY's *hand.*
Were talking—

AMY:

          No, we weren't!

ADAM:

Astonished.

                    Why do you say—

AMY:

Pressing both hands down before her; frowning.
Aunt Mona, it was nothing in particular—
You know, the small talk of woodwork mice—

MONA:

No matter. But I tell you I won't have it.
Felix is a fool about you suddenly,
And I won't have it.

    ADAM *goes to* AMY, *who moves away, her hands over her*
    ears.

FELIX:

                I am a fool. Who isn't?
The world is a dense wilderness of fools;
We stumble through them daily, and thank God——

FRANCIS:

Don't thank God. You don't believe in Him.

FELIX:

Whether I do or not is no one's business—
Yours least of all, lover of yourself.

FRANCIS:

I like myself, as anybody should;

I'm grateful that I am; and grateful too
That all of us are friends here in this room.

MONA:

Friends! If all of us were only that.

To FELIX.

If you were, with Amy.

JASON:

            Why, Mona,
You can't doubt Felix, any more than Francis.
Both of them are bound to you forever.
They can't abandon you; they would be ignorant
Of the first step to take. And I rejoice
That this is so—you know I always have.
My dear wife walks the wilderness of days—
Felix is right, it is a dismal thicket—
With guardian angels paired by Providence
To love her and protect her. Strange, now,
That you should doubt them, one or both.

MONA:

Her excitement rising.

                          Not both,
Not Francis.

FRANCIS:

            Never doubt me, Mona.

JASON:

                    Never
Either of them—I would swear it, dearest.

FRANCIS:

Mona, trust us both.

Waves toward FELIX.

FELIX:

                Stay out of this,
Samaritan. I can take care of me.

FRANCIS:

But can you, Felix? Mona's wild words—

Looks her way, as if in apology, but she does not acknowledge it.

You have not tamed them; sent them back home
To winter in her throat.

JASON:

Good! Then spring——

MONA:

Turning desperately to him.

Jason, how you torture me.

JASON:

Torture!

MONA:

By never being jealous.

JASON:

Jealous?

MONA:

Yes!

As if you were a father, and you had
One daughter—me—whose suitors you indulged
Coolly, kindly, from a noble distance.
Magnanimous, but not my husband. Jealous?
Yes!—oh, but that would warm me, Jason.
Winter—spring—mine is an endless fall.

FRANCIS:

As JASON is about to protest.

The sweet thing, I thought, was that no wrath
Troubled our four waters. We are friends,
And more than friends; the waves run higher with us
Than in the backward bays; yet never a storm
To break us on each other.

FELIX:

Sullenly.

He makes sense
For once.

MONA:

As you do not. And as for Jason—
He wants no waves at all.

AMY:

Breaking with difficulty the silence she has been maintaining.
Adam, you see?
Lovers—friends—I told you.

MONA:

Then you talked.
Was it of us? Impertinent, if so.
What do you know of love that has grown old
And cold?
Looking away.
Or else not cold—oh, no, not cold.
Go somewhere else now, both of you. Dance
To your own music. You can make it up—
Go on!

AMY:

As she leads ADAM, *bewildered, toward the door.*
Just as you say, Aunt Mona, but we meant
No harm. We only wondered if you four——

MONA:

Wonder elsewhere, then.
They go out.
Now!
Her voice rising still higher.
I'm saying
All of it at last. Why did I wait?

FELIX:

A good thing, to wait.

MONA:

You never have.
That sharp tongue of yours goes in and out
Like knitting needles—click!

FELIX:

Mona dear,
Why are you suddenly like this to me?

MONA:

Why are you so suddenly like that
With Amy?

He protests with his hands.

But my subject isn't you.
It's Jason.

Her voice breaks as she says the name, and JASON *starts toward her.*

No, stand there and let me say it,
Now that I have the courage; or the weakness.
I can't face it any more alone.
Of course I know the reason you're not jealous.
You're not in love with me, and never have been.
So you don't care—not with your heart, I mean,
That never hurts as mine does. Mine has hurt
So many years, it should be healed now
By time, by repetition; but it isn't.

JASON:

While all of them, uncomfortable, stare in various directions as if laboring to avoid the appearance of listening too closely.

Mona, what are you saying!

MONA:

You're in love
With Helen—now, as in the beginning,

Helen. Always Helen. She's the one
Woman who could hurt you. But she won't.
Oh, no, you're safe with Helen. She's in love
As I am; only in my case you don't care.
I can't hurt you. How I wish I could!

JASON:

*Agitated, looking at the others in turn; they still avoid his
eyes.*

But you do hurt me, Mona.

MONA:

                              Not your heart.
Your pride, yes—and oh, my own. But pride!
That's nothing. I have thrown mine to the wind—
The birds—anything that flies.

JASON:

                              Darling——

MONA:

Don't say that. Never say that again.

JASON:

Darling.

FRANCIS:

As agitated as JASON.

          He is right to disobey you.
Good words like that are gold; they'll never tarnish.

MONA:

They can be lost, though, like rings. Francis,
What can you know of this?

FELIX:

                              Or I, Mona?

MONA:

You!

FELIX:

With a formal bow, exaggerated.

    Yes, me. Remember? One of your slaves.
One of your three slaves—including Jason.

MONA:

Jason? But he's free. That is my anguish—
Anguish, idiot! Don't you understand?

FELIX:

Now, now! Strong words can be a weakness. Even
Love, the strongest of them all, can be.
What's happened to us here? A stranger's ear
Might call it caterwauling: noise, noise,
At which old shoes are thrown—tin cans—hot water.
But nothing stops it. We must stop ourselves—
You must, Mona. Silence—that's the gold
Was never known to tarnish. Words can.
So no more words. Let's think before we speak.

MONA:

As if you ever did.

FELIX:

              Well, *while* we speak.
That's what I do.

MONA:

              Oh, is it? Then, for a change,
Think while *I* speak; for I have more to say.
Jason, you will tell me in a minute
That Helen is the oldest of our friends:
The very oldest.

JASON:

              From the beginning—yes.

MONA:

And merely that, you'll say. But now last night
I watched you two while the music played——

FRANCIS:

                                        Mozart.
The Countess's great heart was broken, broken.

MONA:

I watched, and what I saw go back and forth
Between your eyes was nothing I have seen
In all of our twenty years. You've never looked
At me that way; you couldn't, had you tried.
Perhaps you *have* tried; but now I know
The secret of your failure—of my failure.
You do not love me; I have never made you
Love me. I have tried, but you don't love me.

> *Stares at him, stunned by her repetition of the words; then*
> *wheels suddenly to the* DOCTOR, *who has been standing by*
> *some framed photographs on a small table, taking one up*
> *and then another, slowly.*

Gail, you were there! You saw it too. You know.

DOCTOR:

Still examining the photographs.

Nonsense.

MONA:

             No, *not* nonsense. All these years
You've known what I have known.

DOCTOR:

                          What's that?
I don't know much of anything these days.
Everything surprises me. What's this
I'm now supposed to know?

MONA:

                     Hippocrates,
Tongue-tied.

DOCTOR:

        Thank you. A good doctor.

MONA:

                      Oh,
The oath, I mean. But here inside my house
You can say all you please: say all you saw
In the old days.

DOCTOR:

Puts down the last photograph.

            Good Lord, what did I see?

JASON:

Mona!

MONA:

   Don't Mona me!

To the DOCTOR.

           Say what you saw.

DOCTOR:

My God, what *was* it?

MONA:

         Why, that Jason wanted
Another wife than me, and for some reason—
Oh, what was it?—had to be content
Merely with me. Not Helen, whom he wanted,
And asking, was refused. Now why was that?
You may not know, of course. But you can say
Helen was whom he wanted—beautiful Helen,
Who has him after all, as he has her.
Why couldn't she forget him and go off—
Oh, anywhere, and leave him all to me?
Why did she not take him when she could?
Tell me that, Physician. Yet she did—
She took him, he is hers. And I am no one's.

FRANCIS:

But you are ours—all of us.

MONA:

I say
I'm no one's. I should know. And I *have* no one.
I've never had Jason. Don't you see?

FELIX:

You heard what Francis said. Or did you hear?
Where are you, Mona?
As if attempting to see someone who has disappeared.
Who is this stranger?

MONA:

Ignoring him, and appealing again to the DOCTOR.
I've never had him. Don't you understand?

DOCTOR:

That's Sanskrit to me. The man has *been* here.
He keeps no other house.

MONA:

As if that mattered.
Doctors are so dense. They seem to see,
But bones is all they show us in their pictures;
And if they take our pulses, only an engine's
There for them to measure, stroke by stroke.

DOCTOR:

Internal combustion.

MONA:

What?

DOCTOR:

Oh, nothing.

MONA:

Nothing! So you put me off, like Jason.

DOCTOR:

Jason? You've had Jason.

MONA:

No! No!

JASON:

Mona, I did marry you; and here,
Happily, I am. We have this house—
No children of our own, but this is the house
I brought you to, with Amy after a while
To sweeten it; thank heaven we have Amy.
Even without her, though, it would have been
My happiness to stay here. I have stayed.
I have been faithful, as you have. We both have.

MONA:

You have been faithful in your fashion.

JASON:

Fashion?
That means unfaithful.

MONA:

With your eyes, Jason.
They have been hers, not mine. Your every thought
Is Helen's—I know that.

DOCTOR:

Second sight.

MONA:

Doctor Dense, *you* wouldn't know.

DOCTOR:

                                    I would,
I do.

MONA:

The vanity of that! Listen.
You only see what others do: a haze
That hangs above, around us. Felix, Francis—
They are the haze.

FELIX:

                    Aha!

FRANCIS:

                    Mona, my sweet——

MONA:

You hear their voices. They are hazy too:
One hard, one soft, but it is all a screen
That Jason loves. He didn't build it—true—
But neither does he *un*build it. Why?
Because it hides the emptiness between
His heart that isn't mine and mine that's his.
A desert there, with sand and rocks. Yet who
Will see it there as long as these mirages
Hover the skyline? He tolerates them
Because they suit his purpose, not because
He's nobler than most men.

        Catches her breath.

                            And yet he is,
He is! If he were only mine.

FRANCIS:

                    He is,
And so are we.

FELIX:

Going.

> Speak for yourself, Birdlove,
Not for me. Mirages! I have heard
Of those things suddenly not being there.
They come, they go. A great pool of water,
With palm trees; then nothing. Let's be nothing.
At least a little while: till Mona, say,
Is Mona. She is not herself tonight.

MONA:

Go on, then. But in what far room you whisper
You still will be a mist before the eyes
Of sensible physicians.

DOCTOR:

> Cataract.

MONA:

So wise, so witty! But the cloud is such
That clear things are unclear, except
For me who now see everything.

DOCTOR:

> Twenty-
Twenty.

MONA:

> Wise!

FELIX:

Taking the arm of FRANCIS, *who resists a moment.*

> Francis, a game of chess.
I've learned an opening——

FRANCIS:

> No!

FELIX:

                              Yes, yes,
Come on.
They go out.

JASON:

      Mona, you humiliated them.
As hostess of this house——

MONA:

                        The ghost of her.

DOCTOR:
Ectoplasm.

MONA:
Furious.
            Still sneering!

DOCTOR:
Over his glasses.
                  Diagnosing.

MONA:
Quack! But I'll expose you. Until then,
Don't you dare deny what I have said
About—well, things!

DOCTOR:

                  De rerum.

MONA:

                        Don't,
I say, be like a low conspirator,
Always at Jason's side, no matter who
Butters your bread; and you know Jason does.

DOCTOR:

*Angry at last, takes off his glasses, folds them into a case,
slips it into his pocket, and stares at her.*

All right, I'll tell you something *you* don't know.

JASON *stirs uneasily, but waits.*

You wonder why Helen wouldn't have him,
As you did, for husband.

JASON:

Alarmed now.

Gail, be careful.

Think a minute.

DOCTOR:

I have. Many minutes.

MONA:

Good! Felix would approve. Go on.

DOCTOR:

All right, then I won't spare you.

FRANCIS *and* FELIX *return quietly.*

Nor them either.

Not that it's anything to them; not
That anything is anything to them—
Tapeworms, hookworms, parameciums.

FELIX:

Thank you, Doctor.

DOCTOR:

Oh, don't mention it.

Still glaring at MONA.

Helen couldn't marry, or thought she couldn't;
And still thinks so, although the evidence
Has shifted a little, Jason being childless.
Whose fault is that?

MONA *covers her mouth.*

Well, who knows?

MONA:

Almost under her breath.

Childless!

DOCTOR:

Now have you guessed?

MONA:

No.

DOCTOR:

Helen thought—
And thinks—she had no right to bear children.
Her mother was insane.

MONA *gasps.*

JASON:

Hippocrates
Is turning in his grave, his Greek grave.
Gail, you shouldn't have published that.

DOCTOR:

Takes out his glasses, puts them on again.

I know.
But Mona made me mad. That's hard to do,
Yet Mona did it.

MONA *stares intently at him.*

The worst thing I said
Concerned you, Jason. What a joke if Helen's
Fear was over nothing!

MONA:

Screams.

Devil Doctor!
I made you mad? You were already mad—

Mad, *mad*. A joke, you say? Doctors'
Jokes—how I detest them!

FELIX:

Or a jest.
Not his, not anybody's. Just the way,
Or one of the ways, the world goes. Ironic,
Rather—I should say ironic.

MONA:

Cold
As ever, Felix.

FELIX:

Oh, my dear, I trust not.
The joke—if that is the word—was not on you.
You didn't think so, did you?

DOCTOR:

Well, I'm through.

MONA:

But I'm not. She could have been his mistress
All the more for this—could have been,
And was. And is. The cream of the jest.

JASON *seems about to speak; checks himself; looks only at the*
DOCTOR. *He does not glance, as* FRANCIS *does, toward the*
door.

FRANCIS:

Helen!

All turn, startled to hear her name, as HELEN *comes rapidly*
into the room, slipping a fur piece from around her neck and
shaking it lightly on the rug.

HELEN:

Hello! It's raining. But not much. I walked
All the way here. Such air! And the pavements shone.

A wet night, but not too wet—that's my
Own hour. You breathe another planet in.

Becomes aware of their embarrassed silence.

But goodness, what's been happening? You all
Seem stricken. Has there been bad news?

DOCTOR:

Could be.

HELEN:

> But what? A war started somewhere?
Someone assassinated? Flood? Fire?
But no, I think not. Every street was quiet;
No one hurrying home to warn his wife
Of the great danger coming or to come.

DOCTOR:

The radio has not been on all evening.

HELEN:

Something domestic, then. I should have called
Before I came—I knew I should have, Mona,
But suddenly I felt like being out,
And where else would I find such dear people?

Hesitates when MONA remains silent.

I know I should make other friends; and do,
Sometimes; but here I know I'll be at home.

Pauses.

Or am I, Jason?

Realizes that he is speechless too.

> Have I come, then,
For once too soon, too often?

FRANCIS:

> You are beautiful
Tonight. The rain——

FELIX:

But even without that——

HELEN:

You both are dears. These are my oldest clothes,
And you don't mind. My walking suit——

JASON:

Speaking with difficulty.

Helen——

MONA:

*Interrupting him almost before he speaks; but her own voice
is strangely quiet.*

My dear, sit down. We were all standing here,
I know, as if a ghost had come.

HELEN *smiles.*

Not now,

I mean, before.

Sinks into the nearest chair.

Sit down, dear, sit down.

HELEN:

Still standing.

No. I'm sure I shouldn't have come. Thank you,
But I'm sure. The very walls are hung
With words not spoken yet; only waiting—
Heavens! Now I know. They were of me;
Or would have been if the subject, like bad weather,
Hadn't herself blown in.

Turns to go.

MONA:

Her voice rising again.

All of you, now,

Sit down! We have the chairs. Felix, Francis,
See that *she* does. Jason, a few drinks?

JASON:

Constrained.

Of course. Helen—

HELEN:

Doubtfully taking a chair that FRANCIS *has placed behind
her.*

Nothing, thank you.

FELIX:

Well,

For one I'm thirsty. Jason, may I?

Goes toward a sideboard where there are decanters.

JASON:

Certainly.

Who else?

FRANCIS *and* MONA *do not seem to hear him, but the* DOCTOR
follows FELIX *to the sideboard.*

DOCTOR:

Spiritus frumenti.

HELEN:

Laughing.

Gail,

You won't let us forget our Latin, will you?

DOCTOR:

Looking back at her over his glasses.

Good for what ails you.

HELEN:

Nothing does.

Unless a touch of guilt—

They all give her, suddenly, their full attention.
                    —for this intrusion.
But I'm not really staying.

MONA:

Shrilly, as before.

                              Yes, you are!

HELEN:

Why, Mona!

MONA:

          Nothing new—you wanted to know—
Has happened. Only the old thing——

JASON:

                              Mona!

MONA:

He must protect you, he thinks.

HELEN:

Stirs in her chair.

                         Protect me?

MONA:

And so they all think. They have sworn an oath,
Probably in blood, to be your knights
And keep you safe from knowing something.

HELEN:

After a second's silence.

                                   What?

MONA:

Knowing that I know. Their oath is really
To keep me from saying——
     Stops abruptly.

HELEN:

With a lightning glance at JASON, *who looks elsewhere.*

Mona! What!

MONA:

Oh, don't you see I see? Tonight your eyes
Avoid each other. That is just the same.
It comes to the identical, terrible end—

HELEN:

Eyes? *N*obody looks at *me*. See there—
Francis, Felix, Jason! If I have
The evil eye, then tell me, one of you!
Jason——

Rises and goes toward him.

MONA:

Stop! I'm sorry!

Covers her face.

Helen, dear,
I'm sorry! You must forget this. Too soon—
It wasn't planned for now.

HELEN:

Turns to her from JASON.

You aren't well.

MONA:

Her shoulders shaking.

I *am* well. I'm strong.

HELEN:

What wasn't planned?

MONA:

Raising her face.

Please forget it all. The old thing—
The new thing—please say you didn't hear me.

HELEN:

I will. But you must promise to let me help—

MONA:

Screams.

No!

Appalled by her intensity, all remain as if paralyzed in their places until voices are heard outside the door, and AMY *comes in pulling* ADAM *by the hand.*

AMY:

Look, Adam, Helen's here! Good!
At a loss because nobody seems to be listening.
                                    Well,
We're going to be married. We've decided.

HELEN:

The most relieved of them all, goes quickly to kiss AMY.

Sweet child—sweet children—this is wonderful.

FRANCIS:

They love each other absolutely. So,
It's natural, this end.

ADAM:
                          End?

FRANCIS:
                      Beginning,
Of course. But the end of music without words.
May all your words be musical themselves.
Felix——

FELIX:

    Don't prompt me. I will make my speech
After deliberation.

    Looks hard at AMY.

          It was necessary,
Deciding. That must come before the doing.

MONA:

What are you muttering?

    Goes to them both, kisses AMY, *takes* ADAM's *hand.*

          Children, be as happy
As anyone ever was, forever and forever.

    Her voice fades with the last three words, and she turns back
    abruptly.

AMY:

Aunt Mona—

    Follows her, takes her shoulders, turns her around.

    —be my mother all that time.
You always have been—

    Hugs her.

          —let it be no different.

MONA:

    Abstracted.

Yes, Amy, yes. Adam, be good to her.

ADAM:

How could I help it? She's so good to me.
All of you have been. You never minded
My coming here so much.

JASON:

    The last to cross over and kiss AMY.

          He seems to say
That's over.

To ADAM, *shaking his hand.*

        Don't turn into a stranger now.
Amy, I am very glad of this.

Kisses her again, on both cheeks and on her hair.

You'll be our daughter always. Don't forget.

AMY:

How could I, Uncle Jason?

Pats his cheek.

                        Doctor Gail,
What have *you* got to say?

DOCTOR:

Comes over slowly.

                 Not much. Let's see—
Virginibus puerisque. How is that?

AMY:

Fine.

FELIX:

If clean.

ADAM:

       Clean?

FELIX:

            I wouldn't put it
Past him to have pulled your leg a little.

DOCTOR:

Over his glasses.

Traction.

MONA:

As the others smile.

       There you go now. So absurd.

DOCTOR:
I make more sense than some.

MONA:

I know. Than me.

Curtain.

Act Two

The same: half an hour later.

AMY *stands at a window, looking out between heavy curtains which she holds apart. She does not hear* FELIX *coming.*

FELIX:
Lucky me!

    AMY, *with a start, hesitates, then turns to him.*

        Sorry if I broke in,
God knows on what fine thoughts—if you were thinking.

    AMY:
I wasn't really. Adam is phoning his mother,
And I was waiting here until he finished.

    FELIX:
Getting her approval?

    AMY:
    Makes a face, good-naturedly.

           I suppose.
I know her, though. We are the best of friends.

FELIX:

Ah! Everybody is everybody's friend.
How lovely, and how lucky. A basket of eels,
Snug and cool together.

AMY:

Shudders.

I've seen eels,
I doubt *they* like each other.

FELIX:

Then you doubt
People. Or some people. Mona—Helen—

AMY:

I didn't hear it all. Oh, I'm so sorry.
Looks out the window again.

FELIX:

And *I* am, because—listen, Amy.
She turns back to him.
I'm lucky—that's my name—to find you alone,
But not because—listen, Amy.

AMY:

Puzzled.

What?

FELIX:

Well, here it is. You can't marry that boy.

AMY:

Pressing herself back between the curtains.
Felix! What do you mean?

FELIX:

Marry *me.*
Now wait. Don't say a word. There isn't time.

Mona was right—she read my mind—and so
Did Adam, who could hardly hate me more
If I had murdered you.

AMY:

Laughs involuntarily.

Oh, Felix!

FELIX:

Funny,
Isn't it? The last thing I'd do.
But let me tell you something that only you
Of all the people here need to be told.
You never even noticed, did you, Amy,
The great change in me? And were too modest,
Even if you did, to think you caused it.
I'm not the same Felix any more;
I don't even resemble him. I care,
Amy, I care. And that's as if a leopard
Had painted himself ivory all over.
Do you know what I mean?

AMY:

Uncertainly.

Care? No.

FELIX:

All things were once the same to me—all things,
And people; none was better, none was worse.
And all, in fact, faintly ridiculous.

AMY:

I see. I rather liked that. It was different.

FELIX:

Please, dear, don't like me as I was.
I'm asking you to love me as I am.

AMY:

Glancing through the door beyond which ADAM *is tele-phoning.*

Love you? But I always have.

FELIX:

No,

Not that way, like an uncle. Don't you see?
I'm serious.

AMY:

Troubled.

Aunt Mona, then——

FELIX:

—was right.

I said she was. But let's not speak of her.

AMY:

Oh, yes!

FELIX:

Oh, no! Or anyway, not now.

It was Adam and you dancing over there
That did it—dancing, singing, touching hands
So lightly, then again—again—again—
That's what made me know. I couldn't bear it.

AMY:

But you made fun of us.

FELIX:

As Francis didn't—

Yes, I know. I had no language then
But that. And maybe I have none now for ears
As young as yours. But understand me, darling,
I'm serious.

AMY:

Takes one step toward him, and he puts out a hand.

Don't touch me. Only listen.

He drops his hand.

Dear, dear Felix!

FELIX:

So you pity me. Please don't.
I'm happy, I am powerful, I am not
The one you think you see—I'm not that one
At all.

AMY:

I see my old friend——

FELIX:

Friend!
So is the policeman on the beat,
So is the postman, so is the President.
It has to be more than that.

AMY:

Looking again toward the door.

It is. With Adam.
Don't you remember half an hour ago?
You heard us; we've decided.

FELIX:

But the doing.
Don't you remember what *I* said? There's time,
There's liberty, to do just what you please.
Not Adam, darling. Me.

AMY:

But I *love* Adam—
Absolutely. Francis said I did.

FELIX:

Francis the sweetsayer! Birdlove—booby—

AMY:

You haven't changed so much.

FELIX:

             I'll take it back
When Francis speaks of you and me that way.

AMY:

No, Felix, no.

FELIX:

        Listen. There is time.

AMY:

There isn't.
Glances once again at the door.
      Now! I think I hear him hanging up.

FELIX:

I don't mean him this minute. I mean you
Forever. You must think of that, my girl.

AMY:

Must? I don't know how.

FELIX:

            Then I will teach you.
Give me an hour—two hours——

AMY:

             But all my hours
Are Adam's.

FELIX:

      Silly thing! You're still the mistress
Of what time is left you in this world.

AMY:

You mean I'm dying, then?

FELIX:

> I mean you're living;
And so am I; we've only just begun.

AMY:

How can I convince you?

FELIX:

> How can *I?*

Looks at his watch.

Listen, Amy. It's not too late. Come with me
To the Black Swan. There'll be a quiet table
Where two like us can talk. I can't say here
The things I ought to—oh, I have such things
To say—

AMY:

> But not tonight! Think, Felix.
Adam——

FELIX:

> Damn that boy!

AMY:

Stamping her foot.

> I won't have you——

FELIX:

Sorry, very sorry.

AMY:

> No, you're not.

FELIX:

I am. Just you see. At the Black Swan——

AMY:

Gestures to stop him; then when he does, steps away and

*stares at him, considering; and finally seems to surprise even
herself by what she says.*

Tomorrow night I'm taking you to dinner——

FELIX:

He also steps away and stares.

No!

AMY:

At the Black Swan.

FELIX:

I'm taking *you.*

AMY:

Shrugs, prettily.

Each other, then. We can say all the things
We need to. This is no place, no time—
Oh, Felix, be my friend, and let me tell you
There and then——

FELIX:

Dejected.

How I'm to be your old
Acquaintance, not forgot.

AMY:

I don't know now
Just what I'll say. But it will be the truth.

FELIX:

And I shall be the wiser for it?

AMY:

Happier,
I hope.

FELIX:

Faith, charity—

Reaches limply for her hand, his shoulders sagging.

                —then shake.

She gives him her hand, which he kisses just as ADAM *comes hurrying in.*

ADAM:

Checking himself an instant.

She's glad. Mother's glad, and sends you a hundred
Kisses.

AMY:

Goes to him and presses her cheek against his.

    One at a time, to make them last.

He tries to hold her, but she pulls away.

Adam, while you talked, Felix and I———

ADAM:

Held hands, I see.

Smiles, to her evident surprise. She presses his arm to show him she is pleased.

AMY:

            Oh, but he kissed mine.

ADAM:

Still undisturbed.

I saw that too. Why not? A gentleman
Of the old school.

FELIX:

Bows, flourishes.

          Sir, your obedient servant.

AMY:

Adam—

    Hesitates.

ADAM:

What, my darling?

AMY:

With an attempt at gaiety.

Felix and I
Are going on the town tomorrow night.

ADAM:

Stands away from her.
How's that?

AMY:

Nervously, rapidly.

We're taking each other out to dinner—
Just for a change—we never did before—
We have so much to talk about, darling—
Chiefly you and me—so new to him,
This business of our going to be married—
He wants to——

ADAM:

Wants to! What does he want to say
That he can't say at home—your home? Or do?
What does he want to *do?* I told you, Amy——

AMY:

Sh-h-h.

FELIX:

Don't shield me. I can hear him now——

ADAM:

Foxes have long ears. Pointed, too.

FELIX:

And so have donkeys.

AMY:

Listen, both of you.

ADAM:

So soon! Hardly had we told the world
When down it fell, a wet tent.

AMY:

Twisting her hands.

                          Nothing's
Fallen. Everything is just the same.

ADAM:

Reflecting.

You may be right. The jungle of this household
Is only a little harder to see through
For one further vine across my face.

AMY:

Aunt Mona?

FELIX:

                She was not herself tonight.
I told her so. But then you didn't hear——

AMY:

Shivers.

Francis told me.

ADAM:

To FELIX.

                    Mona, now. Remember
Mona? What will Mona think of this?

FELIX:

After a pause; examining the rug.

Mona thinks only of Jason. I have wasted,
Such as it is, my whole life. I learned
Something tonight I never knew before,
Or never quite believed. Mona is mad
For Jason; there is no one in the world
But Jason. Francis, too—a pair of fools

Out of some weird mythology: begot
By crook-kneed fawns upon the tenth Muse,
Whose name, I think, is Error. To have believed,
Francis and I, that we made any sense,
Dangling as we did—rivals, too:
Twin puppets on a cord, as like as walnuts
Save for looks; of course he had the looks.
Birdlove is fair of face, of heart, of tongue,
While I am—what you see. My God! Rivals!
We had as much chance, even between us,
As two moths that flutter outside the door,
At midnight, of a marble savings bank.

ADAM:

Assuming that you meant it.

FELIX:

What?

ADAM:

Assuming
Desire, and not its counterfeit—I mean,
The itch to hang on to a good thing.
It's been a life for you—at least for *you*,
Felix. Francis—I can't say; he's pure
Of heart, so may not be a prince of cadgers.

FELIX *turns away, shocked.*

AMY:

Adam, don't belittle all this love
That I have seen my life long. And besides,
There's safety in it for you if it's true,
So why not think it is? Your present danger
Is nothing that can last if he loves Mona—
He still does, I know. He will recover.
Anyway, you're cruel. That's not Adam.
My Adam can't be cruel.

FELIX:

                    He can, and is—

Cadger!

ADAM:

        Parasite, then. Is that nicer?

AMY:

Walks to the door, wiping her eyes.

This evening of all evenings—why, Aunt Mona!

        MONA *enters with such haste that they almost collide.*

MONA:

Addressing nobody in particular.

They didn't even see me!

AMY:

                    Who, Aunt Mona?

MONA:

Why, Jason, Uncle Jason, and——

        Checks herself.

AMY:

                            —the doctor?

He can be rude, we all know know that——

MONA:

                                Oh, no,

Not Gail.

AMY:

        Nor Francis. He would never——

MONA:

                                No,

Not Francis.

        Laughs uncontrollably.

                Francis! Oh, you little goose,

Francis! No, it was Jason, Uncle Jason,
And—well, I went in there to find a book——

FELIX:

One of us does read.

MONA:

                    We all read,
And some of us understand. I went in there,
Thinking to calm myself—I needed that—
And neither of them saw me. There they stood,
Their serpent eyes fixed on one another,
And neither saw nor heard me in the room.

FELIX:

And so you read no more in the book that day.
Were *they* reading, Mona, to each other:
Aloud, and with expression?

MONA:

To the ceiling.

                    Shut his mouth,
Dear God, or else my own.

FELIX:

                    Both would be well.

MONA:

And yet not mine, either. I must cry it
Even to these infants. It was Helen,
Amy.

AMY:

    Helen. *She's* not rude.

MONA:

                    Child!
As if that mattered. No, they stood there, lost
Like lovers in a mist of their own making.

ADAM *and* AMY:
Simultaneously.
Lovers!

MONA:
  Yes, my children, now you know.
Our dear friend Helen, whom we daily
Take into the bosom of this house——

FELIX:
Friend.

MONA:
  Be quiet, monster.
Turns to him.
      Yet I see now
The quaintness in that word. You're not too wrong,
Philosopher.

FELIX:
    Diogenes at least;
Thank you.

AMY:
    But I don't see what they did
Except not see——

MONA:
     Ah, that was everything.
Their eyes, child, their eyes!
  ADAM *and* AMY *look at each other.*
       Oh, not like that.
Or like it—yes—but more so. I can't bear
One moment more of this. I tell you three
Thrice over, I can't live with it and—live.

AMY:
Turning slowly to FELIX.
This was what you meant?

MONA:

Sharply.

When he said what!

AMY:

Why, Aunt Mona, only that you loved Jason
More than the whole world.

MONA:

Wringing her hands.

I do, I do!

Suddenly shrewd.

But why did he say that? To cut a path
Between his heart and yours? Be careful, Amy.

AMY:

I know, though—who doesn't—how you love
The man I too love most, next to Adam.
Not only is he good to me as gold;
He's gold himself, he's lovely.

MONA:

Her hands wild.

Don't, child!

You only twist it deeper in.

AMY:

But Helen——

MONA:

Never say that name again, never!

AMY:

Why, she is my——

FELIX:

—friend. Don't say that either.

AMY:

Slowly.

But *you* are.

*Looks from one of them to the other; walks to the window;
comes back, half fearfully.*

Aunt Mona, would you miss me
If I went out tomorrow night for dinner?

MONA:

Finding it hard to entertain what seems so slight a question.

What? Why, no. You and Adam, naturally——

AMY:

Me and Felix. We've arranged to go.
He wants to talk—well, more than we can here——

MONA:

In a stricken, low voice.

Felix!

Looks about her; grows louder, shriller.

Oh, my God, then I was right!
Not you and Adam. You and Felix——

AMY:

No!

Don't *say* that. You don't understand.

ADAM:

Bitterly.

She may.

MONA:

I do. I understand. I have no friend
Left in the world—not one! not one!

FRANCIS, *coming in, hears this and hastens to her.*

FRANCIS:

                                         You have,
You know you have, Mona. Here I am.

FELIX:

The cavalry at last, and just in time.

MONA:

Francis, dear!

Steps away from him.

                    But what did Felix call you?

Presses her hands to her temples.

Let me remember.

Drops her hands.

                    Lover of yourself!
Yes, Felix said——

FRANCIS:

                    I do not love myself.
I like myself.

FELIX:

                    The officer with his saber
Splits a hair.

Imitates the action.

                    Come now, the difference, Captain!

FRANCIS:

You know as well as I. Love starts at home——

FELIX:

Ah, but liking.

FRANCIS:

                    Liking to be the one
God made you; being pleased with what He did;
And then forgetting that, for there are others——

FELIX:

Don't forget those.

FRANCIS:

Love *is* of others,
But first we like ourselves. Unless we do,
We love nobody else.

FELIX:

I like myself.

FRANCIS:

Do you?

FELIX:

Yes—I think.

FRANCIS:

Good! Good!
There's hope for you.

FELIX:

But others—only a handful.

FRANCIS:

No matter. One's enough.

FELIX *looks at* AMY, *who looks at* ADAM.

Mona, darling,
Don't hate yourself.

MONA:

Myself? I'm not the one
I hate.

FRANCIS:

Then you do hate?

MONA:

You know I do.

FRANCIS:

But not yourself, for what you think is failure?

She stands very straight, staring at him.

Think of me, Mona. I have failed with you——

She gestures to stop him.

Oh, yes, I have. And yet I blame nobody.
Certainly not you; and as for me,
I still like the man you cannot love.
If only you could know him as I do——

Laughs; then realizes how furious she is.

MONA:

Failure!

FELIX:

      See now! The great gentleman
Inflicted pain—was it unintentionally?

MONA:

Both of you be still!

Looks back at the door through which she entered.

              Pain! Failure!
What do you know of either?

FELIX:

Looking at AMY.

                 I can guess.

MONA:

Aware of his glance.

I pray that you will know, in God's time.

FELIX:

Thank you, dearest.

MONA:

            Both of you, I say,
Be still. For I must think.

Presses her temples again.

　　　　　　　And yet I can't.
It does no good to try. And yet I must—
Somewhere I must. Alone, though. No clever
People close around me bearing dishes,
Silver dishes, groaning with ideas.
Runs out suddenly through the opposite door.

FRANCIS:

Poor Mona.

FELIX:

　　　　　　And poor Francis, no true help
In trouble.

FRANCIS:

　　　　　None at all. Still, perhaps—
Starts after her.

FELIX:

Didn't you hear? She wants to be alone.

FRANCIS:

She thinks she does.
Goes out.

FELIX:

　　　　　　Wait! I'm coming too.
To AMY *and* ADAM.
He thinks she thinks she wants to be alone.
I think I know she thinks the worst of me.
Yet what if——

AMY:

　　　　　Felix, dear, do go.
He kisses his hand to her and follows FRANCIS.
　　　　　　　　Adam,
You come too.
Takes his hand.

ADAM:

> She's had enough tonight.
> They shouldn't have followed her that way—the fools.
> No, you and I stay put.

AMY:

> But I know Mona.

Kisses him.

Come, dear, don't let this thing keep us apart.

> *He hangs back, then leaves with her, frowning. The stage is
> empty for a moment; then* JASON *and* HELEN *come through
> the other door, hand in hand, and walk to the window, whose
> curtains* JASON *holds aside so that they can both look out.
> They stand there, still hand in hand but not too close to-
> gether, silent for a long moment, their backs to the audience.*

JASON:

His face still to the window.

Let us not change our minds.

HELEN:

Shakes her head without looking up at him.

> But we know how,
> Don't we? Shilly-shally is your name.

JASON:

No, Willy-Nilly. It is wonderful
To be so sure at last.

HELEN:

> Remember, though,
> How many times——

JASON:

> I don't, I won't remember.
> Not that you ever knew yourself—

HELEN:

I did,
Darling, from the first dance we had—
When you stepped on my foot.

JASON:

Must make a note
To kiss it.

Lifts her hand to his lips.

Meanwhile, lady, will this do?
*They turn and walk freely through the room, sometimes
together, sometimes separately, talking as they walk.*

HELEN:

A hand-to-mouth existence suits me perfectly.

JASON:

Mouth to mouth is better.

Starts toward her; she evades him.

HELEN:

But not here,
Not now. Our last night here—let us be good.

JASON:

And you were going. You thought you had intruded.

HELEN:

I had, you know I had.

JASON:

And it was time—
Our time.

HELEN:

Turns to him suddenly and makes him look at her.

Oh, Jason, *is* it after all?

JASON:

Now there you go. You said you wouldn't change.
Whose name is Shally-shilly?

HELEN:

Mr. and Mrs.—

Both of us.

JASON:

Smiles.

Imagine—registering——

HELEN:

And being shown a shambles of a room.
Think of the rooms we've had.

JASON:

A thousand of them?

HELEN:

Goodness!

JASON:

I remember every one.
I could find my way in the dark, door by door.
The House of a Thousand Rooms—the biggest house
In town.

HELEN:

In the world.

JASON:

Our house. Our world.

HELEN:

And now we're leaving it.

JASON:

We'll have an address.

HELEN:

Mr. and Mrs. Silly Shilly.

JASON:

Laughing.

Silly!
I love you all over again—as always.
You never were the same.

HELEN:

I tried to be.

JASON:

And were—the same and never quite the same.

HELEN:

You, too. I had a thousand lovers, having
You that never changed and yet were new
Like morning over trees, with birds in them.

JASON:

You were the birds. I woke to you. Even
The little birds, that scold. But never me.
You should have, too.

HELEN:

What for? I wish I had.

JASON:

For keeping you out of the world.
Waves, vaguely.

You've had no life
Except our secret one.

HELEN:

Oh, I've been places.

JASON:

Yet where was home?

HELEN:

> Wasn't I welcome here?

JASON:

Yes, but think of the lies; think of the thin
Ice we always walked on, host and guest.
My lies tonight—of course you didn't hear them—
Those were the worst. To her, to everybody.

HELEN:

Let us not think of that; and anyway,
It's over.

JASON:

> So it is, from this night on.

But Helen—let me say it if I can—
I love you—reason sixty—just for this:
That you could be content; that you could love me,
Not in the world's way but in our own,
And never make me guilty.

HELEN:

> For *I* wasn't.

Should I have been?

JASON:

> God, no.

HELEN:

> Then leave it there.

No speeches, Jason.

JASON:

> Nevertheless——

HELEN:

> No, none!

I have been happy. Isn't that enough?

JASON:

*They meet in the middle of the room and he pauses to kiss
her, lightly, before he goes on.*

And I. The wildest dream a man can have
Came true for me—is true. You never lost
The thing I loved you for in the beginning.
Moreover, it increased. Never a day
But I desired you, so that I couldn't wait
Till when I came, and you were there——

HELEN:

And you

Were mine again all over.

JASON:

Looking away, toward one of the walls.

Oh, my stars,
Whichever ones were up when I was born,
That never lost their light.

HELEN:

Oh, my Great Bear
That never swung away from the true North.

JASON:

Oh, Northern Cross, oh, Berenice's Hair.

HELEN:

Oh, Seven Sisters, and the Scorpion,
Pinches him as she passes.
That stings, they say, unless you know a charm.

JASON:

I know one: "God of Galaxies, be good
To Helen, for she is my only girl."

HELEN:

With all He has to do, could He hear that?

JASON:

Yes, if I whispered.

She smiles.

Better than to shout.

HELEN:

So I believe. But something else amused me.
I thought of Amy and Adam, those two blissful
Infants in our midst. They think they have
The secret, being young. What do they know
Of you and me——

JASON:

Oh, they may know.

HELEN:

I mean,
Of what it is to be as we are: born
Each day as if it were the first in the world
Yet not the first either—no, the last
Of a long line that was to this as cold
Dawn to noonday. What do they know of that?

JASON:

Nothing, surely. They are still unborn.
The ecstasy of love as we live it—

HELEN:

Who said that?

JASON:

One of St. Bernard's ancients—

HELEN:

Doubtful.

Ancients?

JASON:

    People, sweet, who lived almost
Forever, and in doing so discovered
That most of us miss everything. The ecstasy
Of those, I meant to say when you broke in,
Would strike these dead.

HELEN:

                       Well—something like that.
Sorry I interrupted you.

JASON:

                 We always
Interrupt each other; we think as one,
So what does it matter which of us ends the silence?

HELEN:

Silence. What is that?

JASON:

              The little wisps
Of time between our words.
    She herself is silent, suddenly, and he stops walking to watch
    her.
                Now what are you thinking,
Queen of the Night, that I am not?

HELEN:

                 Mona.

    He continues to watch her.
We haven't mentioned Mona.

JASON:

             That is true,
And now we must.
    Starts walking again; passes her.
            And yet what is there——

HELEN:

                             Nothing,
Really. But you know I think of Mona
More than of myself.

JASON:

                And so with me.
I don't need to think of *you*; I *know*.

HELEN:

Yes. But what do we know of her? Tonight
Was terrible.

JASON:

         It was.

HELEN:

                Her nights to come,
Her days, when we are gone—can she survive
That silence?

JASON:

             Do you mean, dear, can we?
The thought of it?

HELEN:

            The guilt.

JASON:

Stands very still.

                Remember now
The days of thy creation. You have made
A world for you and me in which no shadows
Lengthened. Guilt was absent from me then
Because you banished it—I said so. Right?
     She nods.
All the while, though, within *this* world
     Gestures about the room.

I lived but half a life. Felix, Francis—
I left the other half to them; they served

As substitutes for someone who was gone.
The someone who remained was more an ass
Than villain: talking nonsense, being noble;
The duke of Heartless House—for oh, my heart
Was where you were. Tonight, however, Mona——

HELEN:

Was not herself, they said.

JASON:

                Or *was* herself—
Who knows? The God of Selves—

HELEN:

                    He's the last God
We meet; and even then He wears disguises.

JASON:

Felix and Francis were as air to her,
Bubbles of air.

HELEN:

       That burst?

JASON:

             Not even that.
They never had been substances.

HELEN:

                Nor suitors?
Once you said——

JASON:

        It was the ass that spoke.
Shaking his head as if to clear it.
And now that he is speaking once again,
He's sick of his own voice.
Resolutely.
        No, my perfect,

The ass is free of his halter. Guilt or no guilt,
I am not changing. We are the ones that matter.

HELEN:

If you were an ass, Jason—I don't admit it—
I wonder what I was.

JASON:

                    I said perfect.
Helen Perfect.

HELEN:

        Ha!

JASON:

               Don't say illusion.
I have none—you know it. All of your faults
Are with you still, and they are what I love.

HELEN:

I've kept certain ones of them so secret—
You'd never guess.

JASON:

             My occupation henceforth—
Here!
    *Seizing her as she is about to pass and grazing with his lips
    over both her cheeks.*

    I'll smell one out.
    A door slams offstage, and she starts away from him.

HELEN:

             Did you hear that?
Someone's coming. *She* is coming. Oh,
Why didn't we leave this house when there was time
And quiet?

JASON:

    Pulling her with him.

There is time. Come on—don't look—
Just come. I'll write the letter late tonight.
Just as we are now—I'm taking nothing—
I brought nothing—hurry!

But just as they reach the door, Mona, Francis, *and the* Doctor *enter through the opposite one. All five persons stand a moment, exchanging glances across the room.*

Mona:

Milder of voice; controlling herself.

Going, Helen?

Helen:

Yes. I meant to before, but we——

Mona:

Had more to say, I know. Goodnight, dear.
Come soon.

Helen:

Looks helplessly at Jason, *who does not know where to turn.*

Mona——

Cannot go on.

Mona:

What, dear?

Helen:

Goodnight.

Mona:

Oh! Well, goodnight again.

Jason:

Conquering a great difficulty.

Mona,
I'm taking Helen home. Don't stay up for me.

MONA:

After a sudden high note of laughter.

Heavens, no! I'm tired. Helen, remember:
I was tired.

HELEN:

Of course—I mean, I'll remember.

MONA:

Breaks a brief ensuing silence.

Goodnight, Jason. Our regular goodnight.
There's time for that, I hope.

JASON:

Crosses and kisses her upturned cheek.

Goodnight, Mona.

Seems to be about to say something else; cannot; returns to
HELEN's *side, self-conscious at every step.*

DOCTOR:

My car's outside, Helen. Drop you off?

JASON:

Gesturing.

No, Gail, she wants to walk. And I do too.

DOCTOR:

Exercise by ambulation. Good.

JASON:

Well, then——

Breaks off and goes out with HELEN; *both of them move
awkwardly.*

MONA:

Dreamily, to herself.

Goodnight, Mona. Goodnight, goodnight.

Alert again.

Francis! Where is Francis?

FRANCIS:

Coming up from behind her.

Here I am.

MONA:

Did I do better?

FRANCIS:

Excellently.

DOCTOR:

Highest

Grade. For what? Was it a test?

MONA:

Oh, Gail,

You'd never understand.

DOCTOR:

Non compos mentis.

Shrugs; goes out.

MONA:

Francis, you said excellently.

FRANCIS:

Clapping his hands.

Brava!

MONA:

I'm really trying, Francis, not to care.
I had no notion it would help so much.

FRANCIS:

You know I've found it so; for if I hadn't,
I should be elsewhere in this lonely world.

MONA:
Lonely? For you? I can't believe it, Francis.

FRANCIS:
Oh, yes, away from you—

MONA:
                              But there are others.

FRANCIS:
None.

MONA:
Thinking a moment.
      Then you do care.

FRANCIS:
                        No, I practice
All that I preach. I keep my self-regard
So high—
      Smiles.
            —dear me, I almost pity those
Like you who do not share that estimate.

MONA:
Like me. Then there *are* others.

FRANCIS:
                              None.

MONA:
Looking back at the door through which she entered.
                              Now Felix.
What supports Felix? You are both
My dears—you know that. But—well——

FRANCIS:
                              Felix.
Self-regard with him is an old habit.

I think the man was born—if he *was* born,
If he was ever young—despising God
For not being greater than He is.

MONA:

No, no!

FRANCIS:

   Well, then, all other visible creatures
For being here at all: poor things at best,
Yet somehow—strange—surviving on
As if they had the right to.

MONA:

        You are hard
On Felix.

FRANCIS:

   He prefers it. And he knows
How much I like him.

MONA:

       He was hard on you.

FRANCIS:

He knew I didn't care. Which is why
He admires me; for I think he does.

MONA:

         He does,
Behind your back.

FRANCIS:

    And tolerates a rival——

MONA:

Sh-h-h. Remember, I don't like such talk.

FRANCIS:

We both know it's hopeless.

MONA:

Think of the years——

FRANCIS:

I've never counted them——

MONA:

—when you've done nothing,
Either of you.

FRANCIS:

Nothing but adore you,
Mona. That was something. That was all.
But Felix—*you* were hard on *him* tonight.

MONA:

I know I was, and I must make amends.

FRANCIS:

You cared about Amy.

MONA:

Yes—for Amy's
Sake.

FRANCIS:

Not yours?

MONA:

Well—yes; a little.

FRANCIS:

A lot, it sounded like.

MONA:

Oh, dear, oh, dear.
Considers.
A lot, then.
Still considers.

So I must make amends
To me?

FRANCIS:
Joyful.

Excellent once more! You learn
Like lightning, dearest one.
Checks himself.

If you *do* learn.

MONA:
Now what——

FRANCIS:

I mean, if you are not pretending—
As Felix would say, putting on an act.

MONA:
Just let him say it!

FRANCIS:

He's not here.

MONA:
Strikes her head.

God!
I learn the lesson, then he says I cheated.

FRANCIS:
To learn it well takes years of doing without.
Not in one night, not in one hour, can pain
Like yours be put away. Not even with luck
Can the lady keep from falling the first day
She tries the tightwire—
Gestures.

catch her there, you clown.
Continues to address an imaginary clown.

Oh! So you love her too. Well, we all do;
But you stay here between her and the ground—
Look! She slipped again.

MONA:

Am I that clumsy
Woman?

FRANCIS:

You are Mona. You can do
Miracles by trying, trying, trying,
And never looking down.

MONA:

Oh, is that bad?

FRANCIS:

Certainly. You keep your head in the air
The whole way across; and think how good
It is to be yourself alone up there,
Balancing forever—ever—ever——

MONA:

An act, after all.

FRANCIS:

But not to deceive.
Only to be. Being is what takes practice.

MONA:

So does deceiving.

FRANCIS:

Ah, but that has a purpose.
This is its own reward; and in the end
No one can take it from you.

MONA:

Starting for the door.

Must I love her?

FRANCIS:

Who?

MONA:

Why, Helen.

FRANCIS:

That is for God to do.
Meanwhile there is someone just as hard,
And you know who.

MONA:

Dreamily.

Myself. Myself. Myself.

Curtain.

Act Three

The same. The following evening, at ten o'clock.

ADAM, *alone on the stage, keeps moving aimlessly about:
paces the floor, goes to look out the window, sits in all the
chairs and on the sofa, picks up magazines and puts them
down, stares frequently at the clock, taps the barometer, and
goes at last to the hi-fi set in the corner, looks down at it a
long time, puts on a record, starts playing it, but soon stops
it, returns to the window, looks out—and wheels to the center
of the room, where he stands watching the door. A moment
later* AMY *and* FELIX *enter.*

AMY:

*Goes at once to him, kisses him, and puts her arms around
him, ignoring the fact that his arms hang down as if he were
not aware of what she is doing.*

Adam, here we are, as safe and sound
As if we never had gone.

    Waits, then walks away a little distance.

                Have you been home
All evening?

ADAM:

Hoarsely.

  Home?

AMY:

   Here.

ADAM:

     Where do you think?

Hello, Amy. Felix.

  FELIX *waves soberly*.

AMY:

Anxious.

    Where's Aunt Mona?

ADAM:

Somewhere in the house.

AMY:

     How's Aunt Mona?

That's what I should have asked.

ADAM:

       You left her.

AMY:

I know. But not for long. I stayed with her

Until——

ADAM:

   Did you enjoy your dinner?

AMY:

       Yes.

But Uncle Jason—did he call?

  ADAM *shakes his head*.

     Or come?

ADAM *shakes his head again, more slowly.*
Or send a note?

ADAM:

Not yet.

AMY:

Oh, dear. I'll go——

ADAM:

Stepping in her way as she starts for the door.
Not yet. Did you enjoy your conversation?

AMY:

Yes.

FELIX:

Adam, here is Eve—intact,
Untempted.

ADAM:

What?

FELIX:

I said, untempted. Once
Away from you, she had no ears to hear.
So she heard nothing.

ADAM:

Relaxing a little.

Did you talk at all?

AMY:

Oh, yes, of everything.
Pauses.

Of Aunt Mona.

ADAM:

She is remarkably quiet.

AMY:
                    Francis?

ADAM:
                         Yes,
He keeps her quiet. He never leaves her; never
Lets her cry.

FELIX:
          Perhaps he should.

ADAM:
                              Perhaps.
But no tears.

AMY:
          Or rages?

ADAM:
                    No. Perhaps
There should be.

FELIX:
               Adam, you are not so young.
How do you know that?

ADAM:
                         I *don't* know—
For sure.

FELIX:
          Older yet. Forgive my ever
Thinking you and Amy——

ADAM:
                    Well?

FELIX:
                         I told you—
Entirely yours.

ADAM:

Going to AMY *and taking her into his arms.*
          Darling, if I waited,
It only was for words.

AMY:

                    And now?

ADAM:

                              I love you.

AMY:

Of course you do. And it is even better,
Now that you did wait. Forever and ever,
Adam, I love *you.*

ADAM:

                    I know it.

AMY:

                         Do you?
Forever and ever?

ADAM:

                    And ever.

AMY:

Silent a few seconds.

                    Where's Aunt Mona?

ADAM:

Releases her.
Somewhere. She and Francis——

FELIX:

Stirs, tentatively.

                    I'll go look.

AMY:

For you and me. Thank you—that's a dear.

ADAM:

Not that she's hiding. She is not ashamed.

FELIX, *listening to this, goes out.*

AMY:

Her back turned for a moment.
I still can't believe it.

ADAM:

But it's true.
The police says that no one was run down.
No accidents.

AMY:

Adam! Did they *report* him?

ADAM:

I did. Nobody knew. She wouldn't have wanted——

AMY:

Of course not.
Her shoulders shake, and he goes to comfort her.
Oh, sweetheart, how could it be?
They were like us, I thought. Uncle Jason,
Aunt Mona—they were like us.

ADAM:

Hesitating.

They weren't, you know.

AMY:

Turning on him.
What do you mean?

ADAM:

They couldn't have been.

AMY:

You knew?

ADAM:

Not until now—tonight. I'll never leave you
As he did her.

AMY:

As I did you tonight?

ADAM:

You told me. And gave a reason—such as it was.

AMY:

No more of that.

ADAM:

No more. But Jason lied—
We heard him: "Don't stay up." We'll tell the truth,
No matter what things happen.

AMY:

Nothing will happen.

ADAM:

Who knows?

AMY:

Now don't be old before your time.
Felix was flattering you—and that won't hurt
As long as you don't inhale.

ADAM:

Smiles.

Who knows, though,
One moment of the future? Moles and men
Are more alike than men admit; the tunnel
Of time is dark for both at the far end.

AMY:

Why, Adam, how you talk!

ADAM:

How do I talk?

AMY:

Like Felix—may I say that?

ADAM:

Shrugs.

Jason and Helen—

It could be we're like them. May I say that?

AMY:

Turns away, her hands behind her back.

I've thought of it myself.

ADAM:

Have you then?

Starts walking, and so does she; they meet and pass as JASON *and* HELEN *did in Act Two.*

You know, we often think of the same things.

AMY:

At the same time. We always do. That's how
I knew we loved each other.

ADAM:

Those two,

Wherever they are—and I don't think they care—
Are just like us; I've noticed; they don't need
To talk; they know.

AMY:

They never tire each other.

Every meeting is as fresh—

ADAM:

                    —as Friday
After school—remember how that was?

AMY:

Oh, yes; it was the time of times.
     Stops as she is about to pass him; and he stops.

                         But Adam!
What are we saying? Whom are we forgetting?
As if those two—how horrible—were right,
And my Aunt Mona wrong. Why doesn't Felix
Bring her?
     Both look toward the door.

               Yet why should he?
     Kisses him swiftly.

                         I'll go find
My foster mother. She was gold to me—
Is gold—and lovely.
     As she runs to the door it is pushed wide open and MONA
     enters, followed by FRANCIS *and* FELIX.

MONA:
Quietly.

               Who is lovely?

AMY:
Embracing her.

                         You—
Why, you, of course!

MONA:

               There, there!
     Kisses both her cheeks.

                    You're home again.
I missed you.

AMY:

It was terrible to leave you.

MONA:

No, for you had promised.

AMY:

But——

MONA:

Had promised.
Always do what you have said you would;
That's everything. Not everybody does it.
Tell me, dear, you will.

AMY:

Tearfully.

I will, I will!

MONA:

Felix found me, and I came at once.
You sent him——

AMY:

No. He wanted—and I wanted——

MONA:

To see if I survived.

AMY *shakes her head.*

Oh, but you did.
Well, here I am—with Francis, who will survive
The whole world, I think. Whatever happens,
He'll be there, still standing by himself.
Even if he's dead he won't fall over.

Laughs a little nervously, seeing that AMY *is shocked;*
FRANCIS *merely smiles.*

Now that's extravagant, but then why not?
These are extraordinary times.

FELIX:

They are.

MONA:

Turning to him.
Felix, I was bad to you last night.
Forgive me.

FELIX:

An extraordinary night.

MONA:

Who made it so? I did. I cared too much——

FELIX:

Perhaps I did.

MONA:

Please let me finish this.
I cared too much about what you saw fit
To do; as if you weren't a free soul.

FELIX:

I'm not one, I am bound to you again.

MONA:

Don't say that, Felix.

FELIX:

Leave me free to be so.

MONA:

Aha!

FELIX:

Aha, indeed. I'm nothing at all
If I can't be a logician. Leave me logic,
And you can have the rest of this queer world.

MONA:

Queer? It's worse.

FELIX:

          No. And *that's* not bad.
Think if it made sense. The very thought
Destroys me. No surprises; no defeats,
No victories; all ends the expected ones;
Nothing to grumble at—or to rejoice;
Nothing to make me cry incomprehensible!
I don't *want* to understand the world—
The vanity of that!

FRANCIS:

          Felix is right.

FELIX:

Thanks, old boy. And by the way, you did
This evening's duty better than I could
Had I stayed on the ship. I went ashore
And made one new acquaintance: a grown woman
Whom I had thought a child. She's going to marry
A grown man: one that has grown old
Beyond his years. I trust the pair of them
Don't sink into decrepitude too soon—
Ancients in our midst.

AMY:

          Why, Uncle Felix!

FELIX:

There! I'm uncle now. So *I* grow old.
It's catching.

MONA:

Sighs.

          So it is. Remember She,
The African immortal?

Shivers.

                    But all at once
She withered.

  Recovers.

          Felix, Francis, you are free
To leave me in the mountain; but I wish
You wouldn't—yet.

  FRANCIS:

                    We never will.

  MONA:

                              Oh, yes,
In time. But now I need you both: one sweet,
One bitter. Which is which?

  FRANCIS:

                    I'm bitter.

  FELIX:

                              So,
By God, you are. You never chide the world
For being—well, the world.

  FRANCIS:

                    What could it be?

  FELIX:

That's it. You take the medicine of life
As if it were a syrup, knowing well
It's poison.

  FRANCIS:

          In small doses. Then it's sweet.

  FELIX:

My very point. You let the bitter be.

MONA:

Children, children!

ADAM *and* AMY *come toward her.*

Oh, I don't mean you.
I mean these boys, that bicker. Keep it up,
Of course—go on—it's music to me. Francis,
How can you say bitter?

FRANCIS:

I didn't mean it;
But then I did; I do. Felix is right.

FELIX:

Thanks, old wormwood.

FRANCIS:

Nodding.

That's the drink I put
To Mona's lips.

MONA:

And never called it wine.
I drank it and I liked it; I am well
Because I took it.

FELIX:

Medicine—my word.
But are you well?

MONA:

I said so.

FELIX:

Really well,
I mean.

Hesitates.

You haven't heard?

She shakes her head.

                    What if you did?
What if word came that every day would be
Like this one?
She stares at him without expression.

              Save for the wondering, the waiting.
Not even that, then. Nothing at all.
MONA *sways perceptibly, but is silent.*

AMY:
Felix, no!

FELIX:
          Why not? Leave Mona to me.

FRANCIS:
Goes to stand by AMY.
He's right, my child, my woman grown. He's right.

AMY:
It's torture. I can see.

FRANCIS:
MONA *listens.*

                    You should have been
With Mona as I have; from room to room,
From hour to hour. I said worse things than Felix—
Supposing those were bad. I made her look
Straight into nothingness—look hard, as for
A mirror that wasn't there. And then one was:
Herself, as faint at first as water seen
In water, glass in glass.

AMY:
                    Why, that's nothing.

FRANCIS:
So it seemed. Yet when she saw herself,

And said "Then this must do," I knew the end
Had come: henceforth no hope, and since no hope,
No anger, no self-blame.

MONA:
                              You see, child—
For still you are my child—he made me young
As you: not in my bones but in my brain.
I'm starting over now, to live alone
And like it. Francis, Felix—even those
No longer are necessities for me;
Although I need their company awhile,
Till I walk better. See?

> *She takes a few steps, bravely, then collapses, sobbing, on the
> sofa.*

AMY:
                              Francis! Help her!

> FRANCIS *does not move.*

Felix! Don't you see?

> *When* FELIX *does not move, rushes to the sofa, straightening*
> MONA's *dress and caressing her back.* MONA, *without raising
> her head, continues sobbing.* ADAM *follows, slowly, and
> stands by.*

                              Aunt Mona, listen!
Maybe this is better. Don't you mind
If we can hear you crying. Adam thinks,
And I think, it's good for you to cry.

> FRANCIS *and* FELIX, *listening, still make no move.*

ADAM:
We think so. We don't know. But Amy's right—
Be natural, Mrs. Howe. Nobody minds.

> MONA *ceases to sob, raises her head, and with* AMY's *help sits
> up.*

MONA:

Both of you are sweet. Francis—Felix—
I'm sorry. I couldn't do it after all.

Waits.

And yet I may. I still may. All of you
Ignore me for a little while. Discuss
Some fresher matter; you must find me stale.

FRANCIS:

No, dear.

FELIX:

No.

MONA:

But I am. To myself I am.
I bore me.

FRANCIS:

Mona!

MONA:

Smiles faintly.

Isn't that the best?
No act now. It's over, and the people
Are all going home. I wish I could hear them
Talking. "Tiresome woman!" There! I do!
That's what they're saying—or they ought to be,
If honesty is in them, and good sense.
You can't fool all the people all the time.

FRANCIS:

You didn't——

MONA:

Yes, I did. You taught me how.
But that's all over too. I'm drained of it,
I'm drained.

AMY:

>Aunt Mona!

MONA:

To ADAM *and* AMY, *now by her side.*

>Both of you—so sweet.
You want me to feel. But isn't it better
Not to? Then I don't embarrass people.
God knows that is the last of my desires.
The very last—you understand? No more
Desires.

She stares straight ahead, oblivious of the DOCTOR'S *entrance through the door in which he had been waiting while she spoke. He comes forward slowly, nodding to the others, and stands where he can look down on her.*

DOCTOR:

>Hello, Mona.

MONA:

Her eyes travelling upward till they reach his face.

>I was hard
On you, too. Wasn't I?

DOCTOR:

>Hard? When?

MONA:

Last night.

DOCTOR:

>Oh. It's a hazard of the trade,
And I don't notice much.

MONA:

>Thank you, Gail,
But I apologize.

DOCTOR:
                    No need.

MONA:
                    There is—
Much need, as you would know if you were a doctor
Of minds as well as bodies.

DOCTOR:
                    Oh. That.
I leave such things to wiser men, if any.

MONA:
Of minds and consciences.

DOCTOR:
                    You let your own
Work overtime.
        Shifts his feet.
                    Mona, you don't know
Who's in the next room waiting to come in.
I brought him.

        ADAM, AMY, FRANCIS, *and* FELIX *turn as if by reflex and
        look at the door.*

MONA:
        Suddenly stands up, staggers, sits down again.
                    No!

DOCTOR:
                    Yes. I found Jason
And made him come. It wasn't too hard at that.

MONA:
        Looking wildly at the others.
No! Just as I was empty. Now to fill
With what? Oh, I don't know. How *can* I know?
Why should this be when everything was dead

As last year's leaves inside me? Warm, too;
A bed of leaves can be so comforting—
Why did you do it, Gail?

DOCTOR:

I'll tell you after.

MONA:

Francis, Felix, Amy, Adam—tell him
No for me so he can understand.

FRANCIS:

Who would have thought it?

ADAM:

Nothing can be known
Before it happens.

FELIX:

Baldhead!

AMY:

Goes to stand by the DOCTOR.

Doctor Gail—
Is speechless.

DOCTOR:

What, girl?

FRANCIS:

Mona darling, this may be
The time of times. Don't say No too soon.
Surviving this, you may survive forever.

DOCTOR:

Survive? What's that? Who's dying? *Moribundus.*
Shall I go get him, Mona?

MONA:

Wait, Gail.
Francis is right; he must come in; but wait
Till I'm alone. Amy, Adam, Felix,
Francis—even you—please leave me now.
And Gail, don't you come back with Jason.

DOCTOR:

No.
Tres multitudo sunt. I didn't plan to.

While the others go through one door, he leaves by the one he entered. A moment passes, then JASON *enters and stands well away from* MONA, *who does not turn her head in his direction. His first voice is almost that of a stranger.*

JASON:

Gail said I had to come. He found me—us—
This afternoon. He ransacked the city.
Pauses.
He told me you were taking it too well;
That was what worried him. He said——

MONA:

Still looking straight ahead.

He said.

JASON:

I thought I would begin with what Gail said.

MONA:

Did he say any more?

JASON:

Only upon
That point: your taking it so well—too well.

MONA:

How did he know?

JASON:

He said you didn't——

MONA:

Scream?

JASON:
Well—yes.

MONA:

He thought I should have?

JASON:

Would have.

MONA:
I didn't run true to form? I wasn't the woman
You left because she—oh, what did I do!
Puts her hand to her mouth.

Don't answer, please don't answer. I shouldn't have said that,
Jason, please forgive me.

JASON:

When I left—
We left—you were so quiet that I too——

MONA:
So nice, so quiet. And I called her dear.
I told you both goodnight. Was that a shock?
I hadn't been myself, Felix said.
Perhaps I had, though, and this other person——

JASON:
We both speak of it. We both remember.

MONA:
Do you? Were *you* worried?

JASON:

We were grateful.

MONA:

Ah, yes. And that's all right.

Looks toward him at last.

So Gail prescribed
Fireworks.

JASON:

Not exactly.

MONA:

Meaning, exactly.
Well, I refuse the cure. I'll tell him that
When he comes in again. Meanwhile he's waiting
For skyrockets, probably. No skyrockets.

JASON:

I told you we were grateful. It was more
Than that, Mona. We almost wondered whether——

Hesitates.

MONA:

You should have gone? It made less sense that way?
Less excitement, was there? Oh, I'm sorry.

He is silent.

Sarcasm? No, Jason, I mean it.

Pauses; looks straight ahead again.

When will you get your things?

JASON:

Hesitates.

I even thought
Of coming back.

MONA:

> To stay?

JASON:

> Yes.

MONA:

> Oh, no.

With or without her—no. It would be with her
Somehow, wouldn't it? You love her.

JASON:

> Yes.

MONA:

You always have, you always will.

JASON:

> Yes, Mona.

MONA:

I knew it all those years I didn't say so.
And if Gail thinks I should have—why, he's right.
But that's the past. The present moment comes
And goes before we know it.

> *Snaps her fingers.*

> > There! It's gone.

We're in the future now.

> *Pauses.*

> Or I am.

JASON:

And I am not?

MONA:

> Doubtless you are too,

But strange to say, you have become invisible.

> *Looks toward him as if this were literally true.*

I couldn't find you if I tried; and I
Shan't try. When will you get your things?

JASON:

Acutely uncomfortable.

Such haste——

MONA:

Haste? What's wrong with that? What you did,
Jason, you did quickly.

JASON:

No. It was long and hard.

MONA:

And yet you did it.

JASON:

Yes.

MONA:

Then let it be.
When will you get your things?

JASON:

I'll send for them.

MONA:

Good. Somebody here can find them for you.
I can't, you know. They're past and gone,
As you and Helen are.
Pauses.

I said her name,
So I remember it.
Pauses again.

Will you be happy?

JASON:

Yes.

MONA:

Good. Now, as you go, send Gail in.

JASON:

Takes a step toward her; stops.
Goodbye, Mona.
She ignores this.
You won't see me again—
Unless——

MONA:

Unless! But I don't see you now.
You're past and gone.

JASON:

Going.
Goodbye?
She stares straight ahead; seems not to hear.
Well, then—goodbye.
Goes out; a door is heard closing; and the DOCTOR *comes in quietly, his eyes searching* MONA's *face.*

DOCTOR:

Was I a fool to do this?

MONA:

Her animation no longer suspended.
Certainly not.
I'm glad he came. We settled certain things.

DOCTOR:

You did, did you? What, for example?

MONA:

Oh,
Certain things—none of your business, Gail.

DOCTOR:
I see.

MONA:
You don't see. But what does it matter?

DOCTOR:
Sits beside her on the sofa, looks at his watch, and lifts her hand to take her pulse.
It may not matter at all if this is good.
After a moment.
It is. Very good. Hm! Remarkable.

MONA:
What did you expect? Roman candles?

DOCTOR:
What?

MONA:
Forget it. An obscure allusion.

DOCTOR:
Roman, though. I flatter myself I know—

MONA:
You wouldn't know this. It's modern. Gail, dear,
Why were you worried? Jason said so.

DOCTOR:
                                        Well,
I was—the way you held yourself in.
I thought it might be better——

MONA:
                              To blow up?
But I did that last night.

DOCTOR:

Before you knew—

MONA:

Oh, I knew then. I was terribly slow about it,
But then I really did. Isn't it strange
That I could have lived alone all of those years
Without quite feeling it? That was the time
My doctor should have wagged his head. Not now.
I am alone and know it. Isn't that good?

He makes no sign.

I feel it, too. Isn't that even better?

He rubs his hands, still silent.

And furthermore, I like it. Isn't that best?

He shakes his head.

No?

DOCTOR:

You wouldn't like it without friends.

MONA:

Ah, friends! But then I have those, haven't I,
Beginning with you?

DOCTOR:

Certainly.

MONA:

Now where—

Stands up and looks both ways.

I can't remember where the others went—
The library, the game room, the sunporch—
Stay here and I'll go get them.

DOCTOR:

No, I'll go.
Sit down again. I'll bring them.

MONA:

Lets him lower her to the sofa.

                              Bossy man.
But you will see I'm mistress here—mistress!—
If nowhere else.

*Pats the cushions right and left, smiling at her hands until
the doctor returns with* AMY, ADAM, FRANCIS, *and* FELIX,
who stand uncomfortably at a distance.

DOCTOR:

                    They weren't far. Eavesdropping,
Probably.

AMY:

          No, no. But Jason's gone!

MONA:

Past and gone.

All look at one another.

                    Come here, you children—
To the DOCTOR.
I had some after all,

          He looks over his glasses; nods.

                    to be my comfort
Until they too are gone. Not past and gone;
Just gone.

*The four, standing in a semicircle, seem fascinated by what
they hear.*

          Francis, are you afraid? Come here.

FRANCIS:

Coming closer.
Why should I be afraid?

MONA:

                    I see no reason,
Unless physicians tremble at the sight

Of patients they have cured—wondering
Who did it: they or the sick ones themselves.

FRANCIS:

In your case——

MONA:

   Myself?

FRANCIS *nods.*

     No, Doctor Birdlove.
You in the first place; I don't forget.
Then me—yes. But after me, Jason.

ALL:

Together, with various intonations.

Jason!

MONA:

  Funny in a way—if ghosts
Are funny. Are they, Felix? You would know.

FELIX:

I doubt it, dear. However, I don't believe——

MONA:

Of course not. But then you never saw one,
Did you? There was one here in this room,
And you know what? It was afraid of me.

AMY:

Going to her and dropping to caress her knees.

Aunt Mona!

MONA:

Stroking her hair.

  Dear!

AMY:

    Don't play with us like this.

MONA:
Oh, let me. Do you know, I've never played.

AMY:
To all of us it's serious.

MONA:
                              What is?

AMY:
That you don't seem to care.

MONA:
                                        Ah, but I do.
I love you all ten times as much——

ADAM:
                                        She means,
Mrs. Howe——

MONA:
                    Aunt Mona!

ADAM:
                                        Well—she means——

MONA:
Oh, I know what she means: I didn't go mad,
And it was madness not to. Is that logic,
Felix?

FELIX:
Delighted, comes up to stand by AMY.
      Flawless, madam. You do well
By all your teachers.
      Walks away.
                              But the school's dismissed—
If I possess authority to say so—
For summertime has come.

Lies down on the rug, sidewise, propping himself up with one elbow and staring trancelike at the audience.

Oh, lazy days,

Oh, sun and grass.

MONA:

Clapping her hands.

The birds are all back—

I hear them—ah, so beautiful.

FRANCIS:

Coming near her at last.

So busy.

To ADAM.

Look, they're building nests.

AMY:

Getting up to stand by ADAM.

Not yet. They're courting.

Nesting makes no noise—why, this room
Is full of noises: crickets, too, and bees.

MONA:

Don't stop them. There will come a time for stillness,
But that's not now; not till you all are gone.

FRANCIS:

Mona, why do you keep on saying that?

MONA:

Because it's true. And truth will set you free—
Felix and you. Don't argue. School is out.

FRANCIS:

It wasn't I that said so.

MONA:

No difference.

It's true. And in the fall who knows what seats

Will be deserted by last April's children?
I see myself alone——

FRANCIS:

No, Mona, no.

MONA:
Queen of myself, and reigning in such state
That some of you will envy me.

AMY:
Dropping to her knees again.

Aunt Mona,
You know that Adam and I will never leave you—
Not really.

MONA:
Meaning really. And you must.
Dear girl, I'll *be* here—where else could I be?—
And you will come as often as you please—
Twice oftener than that, perhaps, in kindness—

AMY:
Kindness!

MONA:
Something so difficult, so rare,
That only you and Adam and Felix and Francis
Have it—oh, I know.

FELIX:
Gesturing toward FRANCIS.

We'll not be gone.

MONA:
You must, I say. Not soon, yet soon enough.
If I'm to be queen——

FRANCIS:
Then who will be your court?

MONA:

Now that's a question. But I don't exclude
You four—oh, from the corners of the earth
Come often, won't you?

Claps her hands again.

Do you still hear the music?
I do.

They stand silent.

Come! We mustn't let it die.
Amy, you and Adam dance.

ADAM *looks at* AMY, *who shakes her head.*

Why not?
You did last night. We heard you. Felix was here—
Felix, dance with *me*.

She suddenly stands.

FELIX:

I'm old and stiff—
An uncle, with a couple of wooden legs.

MONA:

Francis?

He smiles, but bows his apology.

No? But so much music wasted!
It's everywhere, it's in the curtains, even—
See, they quiver with it!

They all look; the curtains do not move.

Vibrate, rather,
And hum, as if a wind were blowing through them,
Plucking every third thread, that hums
And hums—I hear it.

As she speaks, ADAM *moves quietly to the hi-fi set and
searches for a record.*

Adam, what are you doing?

Engrossed, he does not hear her.

We have our own, my dear. We don't need that.

He finds the record and puts it on, lowering the needle carefully.

Our own is of this moment—woven for it
By wind and golden threads. Bird-notes, too,
That break the silken barrier so gently,
You'd never guess their strength. Felix, Francis,
Listen! You won't dance, but you can hear
What I do.

Leans a little.

There!

Waits; and as AMY, *moving like a sleepwalker, joins* ADAM *in the corner, the trio from Mozart's* Eine Kleine Nachtmusik *starts playing, loudly.*

There! That is our moment's
Music. Amy, Adam, dance to it.
The rest of us sit down—quick!—

FRANCIS, FELIX, *and the* DOCTOR *find chairs as she returns to the sofa.*

—that's right—
And let these sweet things dance the past away.

AMY *and* ADAM *have been staring at each other as they listened, and swaying, and moving their feet; now* ADAM *lifts the needle, lowers it again to the starting point, and seizing* AMY *by both her hands pulls her into the middle of the room, where they dance with passionate grace through the repetition of the opening theme, taking turns at improvising the words they half-speak, half-sing.*

AMY:

Sun on the grass,
And grass on the ground,
And you and me, dear,
Dancing time away;
Aunt Mona
Watches—do you see her?—

Watches—oh, I see her—
Dancing with us
In her mind.

ADAM:

Lazy days when
Men lie down and
Birds are nesting—
No, are courting,
Courting, Amy says.

AMY:

Crickets, bees,
And humming birds,
And wind in curtains
Singing to us all;
Aunt Mona
Listens—does she hear it?—
Listens—yes, the dear one
Dances in us
Till we're done.

The music continues while the stage slowly darkens. Those who are sitting keep their positions; AMY and ADAM dance without words until the darkness is complete.

Curtain.

THE WEEKEND
THAT WAS

A Comedy in Three Acts

•

LIST OF PERSONS

In the Order of Their Appearance

STERLING NEUSTADT
MARY SCOTT
MIKE WARLOCK
ROSE LYND
WILLIAM (BILLY) BYRD
ANSON ECCLES
ISABEL JAGGARD
JAMES JAGGARD, *her husband*

Scene

Westchester County, New York. *A room in the country house of* JAMES *and* ISABEL JAGGARD.

Time

The present.

Act One

A large room, expensively furnished, in the country house of JAMES JAGGARD. Doors right and left. In the center, rear, a wide, high window through which the late afternoon sun pours colored light from maple trees in autumn foliage.

NEUSTADT stands with his back to the audience, looking through the window. He is spare and straight, and perfectly motionless even for a few minutes after MARY and MIKE come in. They do not notice him at first, engrossed as they are in a dispute whose beginning words, unintelligible because they both shout at the same time, have been audible offstage.

MARY:

Comes in backward, still shouting at MIKE beyond her. Tears off her bright-red beret, looks for a place to lay it, is impressed by the elegance of the place, and continues to hold it in one hand as she slaps it against the palm of the other. MIKE, glancing swiftly about the room and up at the ceiling, is inattentive for a moment.

Listen to me, Mike. Louis Quatorze
Slept here—oh, yes, and Madam What-do-you-call-her.

221

MIKE:

What do *you* call her?

MARY:

Madam La Whore. Why not?

NEUSTADT *turns quietly and stares at her through glasses
without rims. Neither is aware of him yet.*

MIKE:

Why not? Why not? Madam Why Not—that's you.

MARY:

OK. Why not consider my life too?
My God, the way you drove!

MIKE:

We got here, didn't we?
You seem to be alive—just seem——

MARY:

What's that?

MIKE:

Yak, yak!

MARY:

You disregarded every Stop sign,
As if you couldn't see. Or couldn't read.
Can you read? I wonder.

MIKE:

I can see,
As you can't, when there's nothing in a book.
That bilge you recommended to the boss—
Stinko's novel—how can I push that?
He'll take your word for it, then turn to me:
"Mike, get behind it—big!" A ball of fluff—
Puff, and it disappears. The life I live——

MARY:

Or seem to live. Just seem.

MIKE:

What's that?

MARY:

We're even. I was thinking of your clothes.
To look like *that* in *this* place. I'm embarrassed.

MIKE:

As if you owned me.

MARY:

Well, I do. Or will.

Runs to him and kisses him.

MIKE:

Pulling at his jacket.

Now that's more like it, Mary.

Looks around the room again.

Whew! Where are we?
Whose castle walls are these? The splendor falls——

MARY:

The leaves, the leaves! You wouldn't look at them.
Nothing but the road—a blind man driving.

MIKE:

In an affected voice.

The autumn foliage! Oh, my dear, how lovely!

In his own voice again.

There's nothing new in that. For God's sake, Mary,
What's got into you? Are you my girl,
Or some club lady—

Resuming the affectation.

Oh, my dear, the leaves!

MARY:

Turns and waves toward the window.

But look, Mike! The way the color comes——

Breaks off as she notices NEUSTADT.

Oh! We didn't see you. Or I didn't.

MIKE:

Trying to appear less startled than he is.

I didn't either. Who are *you?*

MARY:

Mike!

MIKE:

I mean, I'm Warlock—Mike Warlock.

Gesturing.

Mary

Scott. Another guest, of course. We didn't

See you, or——

NEUSTADT:

Smiling primly.

But I enjoyed you both.

I'm Sterling Neustadt.

A pause. The name means nothing to them.

Don't apologize.

I seldom go where people speak as you do—

Young people. Modern people. I've been told

I ought to, though, and now I have. Continue.

MIKE:

As both stare at him.

Modern!

NEUSTADT:

Yes. Angry. All the time

Angry, at much or little. Perhaps at nothing.

MARY:

Angry! It was something.

NEUSTADT:

Several things.
His driving, and his clothes; and then a book;
And finally, the leaves. You see, they've changed.

MIKE:

Sarcastically.

Have they?

NEUSTADT:

Certainly, as all things do.
I take it you are publishers.

MARY:

We slave
For one.

MIKE:

And what are you?

NEUSTADT:

It would take time
To answer that. Say, though, I'm a student
Of change—oh, not of leaves. Mr. Warlock's
Right. All Octobers are the same.
I mean society.

MIKE:

Good God. Then we are specimens.

NEUSTADT:

Precisely. Please don't mind. It is my business.

MIKE:

Business?

NEUSTADT:

In a way. There will be leisure
To tell you more about it.

MIKE:

Will there? Well,
I'm wondering what goes on here. Have you seen
Our hosts?

NEUSTADT:

No. A servant sent me in.

MIKE:

A butler, I would say. We ran him down
And walked right over his polite remains—
Backward, in Mary's case. But she was mad.

MARY:

I wasn't.

MIKE:

Don't be idiotic; don't
Deny your woman's birthright.
    To NEUSTADT.

But society.
What's that? You mean this madhouse?
    NEUSTADT *looks about the room.*

Not just *this.*
The whole world—out there—
    Waving.

in here—all of it,
At least as it is run by those that run it.

NEUSTADT:

And *is* it run?

MIKE:

You bet.

NEUSTADT:

By him? By Jaggard,
Our good host? But where *is* Jaggard?
I quite agree, it's strange he didn't greet us.
You know him well?

MARY:

Oh, hardly at all.
Or Mrs. Jaggard, either. One wild night
We went out on the town, and at some bar
We met them. So they took us to their table,
And what do you think? Pheasant!

MIKE:

Feathers and all.

Holds his head.

Oh, what a night! My Uncle Lem had died
And left me—what do you think? A hundred dollars!
He measured me and found me wanting that.
Well, it wasn't enough to start a hospital,
And not much more than enough to stick in my ear.
So Mary helped me blow it in like blear-eyed
Beggars. The Jaggards thought we were specimens too—
Of what, God only knows. So then this weekend,
Such as it is. Doubtless you know him better.

NEUSTADT:

Shakes his head.

He thinks he knows my mind. I don't know his—
Not yet. He read some articles I wrote.

MIKE:

An author.

NEUSTADT:

Not of books—not yet. He sent a note,
Asking me here. I've never even seen him.

MIKE:

Say! What *is* this? Who is *he?* Rich,
That's obvious. But how?

MARY:

He's a collector
Of specimens.

MIKE:

I doubt it.
ROSE *and* BILLY *come in quietly.*
Well! Who's *this?*
More of the same? Or are you junior Jaggards?

ROSE:

Laughing.
Thank you. I am only Rose Lynd.
I work for Mr. Jaggard. His receptionist.

MARY:

With a mincing, artificial smile.
How nice! I'm Mary Scott. This is Mike Warlock,
And that is Mr. Neustadt.

ROSE:

How do you do?
And this is Billy Byrd.

MIKE:

Not in a cage?

ROSE:

Oh, no, he's free—the only man I know
That is. Billy's a poet.

MIKE:

With an income?

BILLY:

Well——

ROSE:

But where is Mr. Jaggard?

NEUSTADT:

As ECCLES *enters.*

Is this——?

All of them turn and look at ECCLES.

ROSE:

Laughs.

No, that is Anson Eccles, an old friend
Of his. They're in a club together—aren't you?

ECCLES:

Many a meal we've had—grand ones, too—
In a far corner of a lonely lounge
Where he and I can talk our very souls out
Before midnight and after.

ROSE:

Souls?

ECCLES:

Why, yes.

Does that surprise you?

ROSE:

Glancing at BILLY.

A little.

MIKE:

Has noted the glance.

Would *he* know?

Poets have no corner on the soul.

BILLY:

That's right, of course. No one has.

MIKE:

Nodding.

                     Now income.

You'd better have one. And a printing press.
Publishers won't publish you. Or will they?
Any luck so far?

BILLY:

                     None at all.

But then I haven't tried very hard.
I'm not sure I'm ready.

MIKE:

                     Don't try me.

I do publicity; but not for poets.
The one attempt I made—

Shivers.

MARY:

                     Mike, don't panic.

To the others.

The very presence of a poet scares him.
He seems to think they have some power—

ROSE:

                     They do.

But not on weekends. You won't be approached.

MARY:

If anybody would, it's me. I'm editorial;
I'm the rejector.

MIKE:

                     Hail to thee, Rejectress.

And still you let too many things slip through.

To the others.
Of the making of bad books there is no end—
We know. What an occupation! Pimps
To poverty of mind. And as for soul—

Holds his nose.
It stinks, these lousy days. I am ashamed
Of what I do. The only worse thing
Would be to *write* the drivel I promote.
I can't afford an author's moratorium;
Still, I'm for it. I'd starve cheerfully.

General laughter.
No, I'm serious.

BILLY:
                Good. I might be ready,
Say, ten years from now.

MIKE:
                Make it twenty.

BILLY:
Very well. I don't intend to die.

MIKE:
Ha, ha, as the first gravedigger said.

MARY:
                Now Mike!

MIKE:
Now mealy mouth!
To the others.
                She's not herself today.
The fact is, she's meaner than I am.
But not here. She brought her party manners.

MARY:
Makes a face at him.
You're showing off.

MIKE:
Damn it, I never do!

MARY:
Oh, no?

NEUSTADT:
Finding it hard to keep his eyes off of MARY.
Let him. I like it. He's a sign
Of something in our times that, till our hosts
Appear, we might discuss.

MIKE:
Boy! A symposium.
Well, let it be in prose.
Studying NEUSTADT.
I think it will be.

ROSE:
Our host—he'll come. I don't know what detains him.
But then it is not so queer: a busy man.
He always does things in his own way;
And this time, perhaps, he has a purpose.

MARY:
Mrs. Jaggard—what's she like?

ROSE:
Thoughtfully.
You'll see.

NEUSTADT:
Now, Mr. Byrd—poetry. I find it
A fossil——

BILLY:
Startled.
What?

NEUSTADT:

       —embedded like a shell
Of some extinct crustacean that the land
Long since closed over. Beautiful back then,
But buried deep now in the world's rubble
We stand and walk on. There is not a change
More clear than this. We have no further use
For song. I speak of change. It is my subject.

ROSE:

Moving nearer to BILLY.
Where do you teach it?

NEUSTADT:

       I don't teach. I do research
For a foundation: an obscure one yet,
But in good time you'll hear of it.

MIKE:

Pulling imaginary bell ropes.
       Bong, bong!
We do already. But now, change. I'd say
Deterioration. That's the program—going
   Points.
Down, down, down.

NEUSTADT:

       Oh, no.

MIKE:

       Oh, yes.
Poetry, for instance. It's a mess,
And everybody thinks so.

BILLY:

Grinning, and putting up his hand like a child in school.
       Even me.

234 MARK VAN DOREN [ACT ONE

MIKE:

Modesty won't save you.

BILLY:

I'm not modest.
I am the only one that's not a mess.

MIKE:

Then why doesn't anybody know it?

BILLY:

They will, after the moratorium.

MIKE:

Man,
Like when? But listen, Billy Byrd. The ones
That haven't knocked the good old Muse to pieces—
Kicked her, slapped her, hammered her half blind,
Then chewed, then choked her—boy, is *she* a mess!—
The ones that haven't are the simpletons,
Singing—I agree with Neustadt now—
Of things as dead as winter flies: of birds,
Of bees, of sheep; of sunsets, waterfalls;
Or else, by God, their girls—there's always that.
Is *she* your girl?

> *Gesturing toward* ROSE.

And if so, are there sonnets
Informing us of the fact?

> ROSE, *close to* BILLY *now, takes his hand unobtrusively*.

ECCLES:

May I say something?

MIKE:

Shoot.

ECCLES:

You didn't mention

The oldest and the newest of all subjects,
The one that can't wear out.

MIKE:

Oh, it's worn out.
Whatever it is. Between the goons and the geese,
The bruisers

Pounds and punches with both hands.

and the breathers,

Suddenly silent, sighs and turns his eyes upward.

every subject,
Punch-drunk, is dead upon its feet.

ECCLES:

Except the one I wanted you to mention.

MIKE:

Well?

ECCLES:

The way the weary world goes,
Changing,

To NEUSTADT.

yes, but always changing back.
The endless repetition—woeful, wonderful—
The same old things, subsiding only a while
Till here they are again: nothing new,
And nothing really old. The world's the same
Forever—fascinating, but it is.
Mr. Byrd—who knows?—he may say that;
Or sing it. Singing it is nicer. Change,
And yet no change. The wonder is the lasting,
For better or for worse. I would say neither.
Better? Worse? Who is there to decide?

ROSE:

Why, Mr. Eccles, you are one yourself.

ECCLES:

A poet? No. I only listen and read,
And nod when something I have always known
Is there to know again. Mr. Byrd—

MIKE:

Don't ask him. He may do it. Shambles of grammar,
Or else the bumblebee, the hummingbird;
Or maybe *her*—

Rolls his eyes.

Ah, but how I long——

BILLY:

He didn't ask me, but I will. Here's this.

Steps back a little, dropping ROSE'S *hand.*

Where she is now
Is where I am.
All of her being
Is my own.

Where I am now,
There she is too.
All of my thinking
Is her thought.

All of our days
So close together—
Ah, but I wonder,
Ah, but I tremble.

Returns and takes her hand, as all but MIKE *clap gently.*

MIKE:

Not bad, not bad. Still, those "ah's." Old hat.

MARY:

Don't be a dog.

MIKE:

                You say such things in letters.
"Dear Sir: We find much merit in your manuscript,
But"—well, what comes next?—"it isn't for us."
And then you can forget the poor guy.
But he remembers those two words, "much merit,"
And back he trots in April.

        NEUSTADT:

                            Spring. Passé.
With all of our houses heated, and the highways
Plowed, there is no season any more.
Birds, yes, and buds; but most of us don't notice.
In the Dark Ages it was a miracle,
And those who had survived till April, sang.
Not now. No song. No seasons. Air-conditioning
Has changed all that. Even the hot summers—

        BILLY:

This last one was, for people out of doors.

        NEUSTADT:

But we don't live outdoors. The country shrinks;
Villages decay, and fields are something
Only to fly over, in altitude-adjusted
Cabins. Even the fields are fewer. Some
Will stay as eyesores: vacant lots
No one can find a use for.
        Pauses.
                            As for love,
That died with song. I mean, Mr. Byrd,
However sweet your words were, they were old
Before Miss Lynd was born; and so was the sentiment.
Two can be one? They can't. Psychology——

        MIKE:
        Holds his head.
Oh, Jesus.

NEUSTADT:

        I mean, Mr. Warlock, each
Is each, and that is all. We have our problems,
But love doesn't solve them. We are alone
Forever, and the wisdom of these days
Is not to fancy otherwise. The song,
The sonnet: they are delicate remains
Of long dead romance. A revolution
Has swept all that away. The age of sex
Is not the age of love, no matter what
One wishes.

MIKE:

        Sex. By golly. Mary, my love—
There! That's the last time I'll say it,
At least in this man's hearing.

BILLY:

                Not in mine.

MIKE:

Oh, no?

BILLY:

        I love not only Rose, but the world.

MIKE:

Some order.

BILLY:

        Yes, but so it is. I love
This terrible world, even though it contains
Monsters like him there.
    Nods sidewise, smiling, at NEUSTADT.
              I can't explain,
But so I do—the whole world, all of it,
Beginning here with Rose and going on
As far as I can see. And I say love.
Why not?

MIKE:

> Go on. Say love.

BILLY:

>> The world is terrible
Because it changes and because it doesn't.
We never can decide which thing we want.
To change or not to change——

ECCLES:

>> That is the question.

MIKE:

Not for me.

MARY:

> Or me.

MIKE:

>> The clock runs down.

MARY:

It's rusty, and the numbers are rubbed off.

MIKE:

Now that's my girl. Dry rot, and savagery—

MARY:

And see the scum that floats on top—the best ones—
Ugh!

MIKE:

> Don't mix our metaphors. The clock——

MARY:

The pot, the cesspool.

ROSE:

>> Gracious!

ECCLES:

                    Or the woman.
The world is an old hag—she is so old,
Nobody knows her age—who cannot die
And never will. Toothless since the Flood,
And tough—beware of her and her nine lives.
She scratches while she purrs. Beware of her.

ROSE:

Then you don't love her?

ECCLES:

                    Dear, I dote on her.
She's all I have—we have—and she's forever.
But she is older than this scientist

Indicating NEUSTADT.

Imagines. She was old from the beginning;
And since I like old ladies, she is queen
Of everything for me. And what a memory!
Changes? She recites them as she stitches:
"This one, that one, t'other—yes, I think
I'll bring that nice one back. But I won't keep him.
No, I'm fickle. It's a crazy quilt
I weave. Come under, children, and keep warm."
Deterioration, Mr. Warlock? Decadence?
No. More and more of the same, glory to God.

NEUSTADT:

God?

ECCLES:

I just happened to say it. Glory
To something, anyway, that won't die.

NEUSTADT:

The world for me is not a person at all.

MARY:

And who's surprised?

NEUSTADT:

It is a drawing board
On which the plans keep shifting: this one now,
Quite handsome; then another—look at that—
But soon it too is slipped away, and a third one
Lies there; yet a fourth is coming fast
To be the one we marvel at. But briefly.
For there are more: infinities of plans,
No one of which is permanent.

MIKE:

Yet better?
Each one better?

NEUSTADT:

Progress, you mean? Oh, yes.
But don't inquire about the end of it.
I can't see the end, nor do I care to.
However, each improves upon the other;
I can see that.

MIKE:

You're lucky.

NEUSTADT:

Error departs
And stays departed. Error cannot return.

ECCLES:

Poor world!

MIKE:

And truth appears.

NEUSTADT:

That is my faith.

MIKE:
Some faith.

To the others.
   Our statistician is religious.
Now tell me this, Neustadt. Fast, you say—
The fourth blueprint materializes fast.
How fast? Is it like a moving picture?
Film after film, quicker than eye can see?

NEUSTADT:
Shaking his head.
Quite relative. The geologic ages—
How rapidly did they succeed each other?
When nothing told the time, each was forever;
Or seemed so. And you can make this true
By trying. A mere glance at the charts
Reduces them to moments. That is false,
But so is it false to say they never were.

ECCLES:
We do have time, then, to get adjusted.

NEUSTADT:
Some of us do. Some of us never do.

ECCLES:
Meaning me.

BILLY:
   No, me.

ROSE:
   No, me.
Voices are heard beyond the door.
   But listen!
They're coming at last.

ISABEL JAGGARD *enters first, followed by her husband. She is
smartly dressed in fashionable sports clothes; is slender and
intense; is beautiful; is predatory in her glances at the whole
company, but particularly at the young men,* MIKE *and*

BILLY. JAGGARD, *in slacks and a plaid jacket, is portly, suave, and self-possessed; as he moves among the guests, greeting them, he seems convinced of his own power and importance. First, however, he waits for his wife to complete her tour.*

ISABEL:

Dear people!

Brushing her bosom lightly with long hands.

               Why, I'm out of breath! Forgive us,
Won't you? There were things outside to see to—
Things we hope you'll all enjoy tomorrow.
But don't ask me what. Surprise, surprise.
Mr. Warlock,

   Goes to him and seizes both his hands.

        you were good to come,

Inclines her head toward MARY.

And bring her too. Such a rare night we had!
We haven't forgotten. No hangovers, I trust.

MIKE, *uncomfortable because she continues to hold his hands, smiles a forced smile and shakes his head.* MARY *watches, all too interested; and looks relieved when* ISABEL *moves on to* BILLY.

And this, Miss Lynd—why, can it be your poet?

Takes BILLY's *hands.*

Let's see how one of them looks.

Steps back, still holding on.

                Not very different.
Should I be disappointed?

BILLY:

             No, Madam;
Unless we all are. People, I mean, not poets.

ISABEL:

Drops his hands, but continues to stare into his eyes.

Good, good! I like that.

Turns.

Mr. Eccles,

I've seen you before. Welcome again.

He bows.

And now the stranger.

Goes to NEUSTADT *and shakes his hand briefly.*

But he won't be, long.

Mr. Neustadt, of course. James, my dear,

He came!

JAGGARD:

Moving swiftly past her, shakes NEUSTADT'S *hand: a formal gesture which he will repeat with all the others. He speaks tersely, with no special emphasis.*

Excellent. We have some things

To talk about.

Proceeds among the company.

Warlock, hello. Miss Scott,

How goes it?

She starts to speak, but he has moved on.

Mr. Byrd, I know your name.

BILLY:

It isn't public yet.

JAGGARD:

Oh, no.

Glances at ROSE.

Quite private.

To ECCLES.

Anson, how do you do?

ECCLES:

Smiling.

As the world goes,

Well.

JAGGARD:

Good, good! As the world goes—
You have the secret of it? You still do?

Turns his back as ECCLES *opens his mouth to reply.*

Isabel, what next? You have the schedule—
Rose!

Goes to her as to someone he has overlooked.

For the second time today—
Significantly.

or the third—
Hello, beautiful.

ROSE:

Embarrassed.

Good afternoon, sir.

JAGGARD:

Sir? Forget that. Here at home I'm James.
James—can you manage?

ROSE, *evidently astonished and terrified, shakes her head.*

Well, try.

Continues holding her hand, to her acute discomfort and to
BILLY'S.

Isabel, what now?

Before she can answer.

You lead the ladies

Slowly withdraws his hand from ROSE'S.

Up to their rooms for a little rest, and a change—
Why not, it's getting late?—for drinks, for dinner.
You do that, and I'll advise these gentlemen——

ISABEL:

Do that.

Motioning to ROSE *and* MARY.

Come with me, then, if you can bear

To leave them—two of them, anyway. You know
Which two I mean. It's hard even for me.
I'm not yet old enough to be their mother.

> As MIKE *and* BILLY *turn.*

Oh, I'm not very old. You'll see, you'll see.

> *A silence as she goes out with* ROSE *and* MARY.

JAGGARD:

Well! Here we are, gentlemen,
Alone, as any man in his right mind
Prefers, at least once in a long while.
Not always, though. That's too much. The flesh
Can't stand it—can it, Eccles?

ECCLES:

               Mortification.
Hardly. There is a time for that. But no,
Not now. There is a time for drinks and dinner,
And looking into beautiful grey eyes.
Miss Lynd—I like her eyes.

> BILLY *looks toward him, somberly.*

JAGGARD:

              Aha! But now—
Well, Warlock, let me warn you. Sooner or later
I have a little something to propose—

MIKE:

To me? Good Lord, why me?

JAGGARD:

                Why not? But later,
After we have eaten. And I hope
You'll like what we've provided, me and my gun.
I have a stock of birds——

MIKE:

             Pheasants?

JAGGARD:

Partridges
And quails, and once in a blue moon, a woodcock.

BILLY:

Cliché.

JAGGARD:

Touché. A lavender moon, then.
So Warlock, you are warned. But gentlemen,
A second reason why you all are here
Just left this room.

They look toward the door.

Rose, you know, is my mistress.

*A dead, shocked silence, broken only by an inarticulate cry
from* BILLY *which* JAGGARD *ignores.*

My problem is to have the time with her
I need, and may I say for her, she needs.

BILLY *moves slowly toward him, like one in a trance.*

Our days are—well, busy. And most nights.
But now the girl is here, and—must I explain?
Mr. Byrd, must I explain?

BILLY:

Stopped in his tracks.

You liar!

JAGGARD:

Now, now!

BILLY:

We *live* together, Rose and I.
She is my wife—almost. I know her better
Than any living soul. You liar! Explain?
What is there to explain?

JAGGARD:

Why, what she does
And where she is when you are writing your damned
Poems. I admit she takes those seriously.

BILLY:

Incoherent.

Where—when—

JAGGARD:

The time, the place? But lovers,
Boy—you ought to know—have many devices;
And every day has twenty-four neat parts.

BILLY:

But don't you see? I *live* with her, I know——

JAGGARD:

There, there! A gentleman wouldn't tattle.

BILLY:

But *you* have.

JAGGARD:

I am no gentleman.

MIKE:

Watching them both with an excitement he can barely control.

Hear, hear!

To BILLY.

Now this is wonderful. Oh, boy!

Recites in falsetto.

Where she is now
Is where I am.
All of her being
Is my own.

Where she is now is where you aren't—or him
Either. Up in Rose's dressing room:
That is where she is, all by herself.
Every day has twenty-four compartments.

ECCLES:

I am the rose of Sharon, I am the lily——

BILLY:

Stop it!

ECCLES:

     Kiss me with kisses sweeter than wine.
My little sister has no breasts——

BILLY:

                          Stop it!

ECCLES:

Perhaps I sing for *you*—with Solomon's help.

NEUSTADT:

Sing? Solomon? Those days are gone.
The sexual revolution——

MIKE:

Holding his head.

                  Oh, my Christ,
Deliver us from all of that. Computer
Cards, with little holes in them—square holes—

NEUSTADT:

All of you might benefit by listening.

MIKE:

Shuffle, shuffle, clickety click.

   To BILLY.

                   Old man,
You've had it, haven't you? Too bad.

A big bang, on both sides of the head.
Or was it like a knife—the jugular?

Hums.

> All of our days
> So close together—
> Ah, but I stumble,
> Ah, but I stagger.

BILLY:

Suddenly more quiet, but in a broken voice.

> Her faithfulness is moon and stars,
> But it was born before they were.
> When chaos still was utter cold,
> All alone she sang to me.
> I heard her even then, and cried;
> And still I do. We never died.

MIKE:

After a general silence.

Never, never, never, never, never.
> I am an unborn calf.
> I cry in there, I laugh.

BILLY:

You are like him.

MIKE:

> The hell I am.

ECCLES:

> You all

Are jesting. There is a time——

MIKE:

> Ticktock.

JAGGARD:

Briskly.

> A time

For dinner, yes. Gentlemen, come with me.

Starts toward the door.

There is a room for each of you to dress in.

MIKE:

Dress? A monkey suit? I haven't got one.
I'd rather wear the emperor's new clothes.
How would they do?

JAGGARD:

                    Amusingly. Eccles?
Neustadt?

NEUSTADT:

           We're provided. Or I am.

ECCLES:

And I. But Jaggard, let me say—oh, dear,
Inarticulate for once.
Miss Lynd—I can't believe——

JAGGARD:

                 Say it later,
Over the brandy. Byrd, I'll lend you something.

BILLY:

Nothing. I'm not here.

JAGGARD:

              But you must be;
We see you.

BILLY:

        I'm not here.

JAGGARD:

              Come, come.
Turns.
                    I'll have
My butler show you all where you're to sleep.
But don't sleep yet.

Consults his wrist watch.

                        Dinner's in half an hour.
Byrd! Come with me.

BILLY:

Motionless.

                        I am not here.

JAGGARD:

Where are you then? Gentlemen, he's gone.
Our young friend is gone. Don't look for him,
He's gone. But you are with me still, I think,
So let us take our separate ways upstairs.

> *Goes to the door; waits; and follows them out as they leave*
> *reluctantly, glancing back at* BILLY, *who seems unaware that*
> *he is being left alone. As soon, however, as the last of them,*
> MIKE, *is through the door he starts walking aimlessly up and*
> *down the room, stumbling over rugs, bumping into walls, and*
> *striking his hands noiselessly together. Then* MIKE *reenters.*

MIKE:

A big, big bang. I'm sorry.

BILLY:

                        What did you say?

MIKE:

I'm sorry. Which is putting it more mildly
Than Jaggard, the big jerk, deserves.

BILLY:

                                        Despise me,
Don't you?

MIKE:

          What?

BILLY:

               You know. The little boy's
Been hurt, and great big man feels sorry for him.

MIKE:

No. Those poems—they're all right.

In mock apprehension.

                                        Now mind you,

No solicitors allowed.

BILLY *shakes his head.*

                    OK.

You pinned your heart on your lapel, though,
And Jaggard took a shot at it.

BILLY:

                            But, Warlock——

MIKE:

Listen.

BILLY:

        No, you listen. Why did he lie?

MIKE:

Waits a second.

Did he?

BILLY *looks squarely at him.*

        Did he?

Waits again.

                    Well, it's none of my business.

BILLY:

Yes, it is. It's everybody's business.
Why did we all come to his damned house?
That's what I want to know—why did we come?
Of course he lied. And why was that? Why?
Why?

MIKE:

Imitates an Indian.

        Careful now. Little boy
Ask questions, great big man he answer—maybe.

BILLY:

What do you mean?

MIKE:

                    Why, nothing, till I know.
I'll wait and see. You do the same.

BILLY:

Pointing to the door.

                                   Go there?

MIKE:

Why not? She didn't hear. Watch and wait—
Man, that's my motto. Come along.

BILLY:

No.

MIKE:

We'll miss you. *She* will miss you.

BILLY:

                                   No!

MIKE:

Afraid of her? Moon and stars—afraid?
Too bad if so, for you convincèd me.

BILLY:

Afraid of evil—I'll confess to that.

MIKE:

Face it, face it! Play the game out, Byrd.
Let's see it to the end, whatever it is—
Both of us. I'm with you.

BILLY:

                    Thank you, Mike.

MIKE:

To the audience.

Look, he knows my name.

BILLY:

But how can I——

MIKE:

Hell, I don't know. But poets are tough people,
And maybe, as I say, it's some new game:
Serious, but a game.

BILLY:

I can't imagine——

MIKE:

There! You abdicate. Imagination's
All you've got, and you throw *it* away.
You mean to tell me you're not even curious?

BILLY:

After a pause.

Perhaps I am.

Another pause.

Yes, I am.

MIKE:

Bravo!

BILLY:

But you go on alone. I'll come in a minute.

MIKE:

Starts away, then stops.

How can I trust you? Minutes can be hours.

BILLY:

Go on. I'll come.

Walks over to the window.

MIKE:

All right.

Is met at the door by ISABEL, *coming in.*

ISABEL:

Oh, Mr. Warlock!

This is wonderful—so soon alone.

Puts her hand through his arm and leads him to the center of the room.

Now!

Turns suddenly and slips her hand down his side, caressingly.

So soon! When was there such luck!

Instinctively he moves aside so that she sees BILLY *behind him. She is not confused.*

Mr. Byrd, too. What shall I say?
Two in a bush?

MIKE:

Claps his hands, affectedly.

Clever, clever!

Looks at his watch.

It's late,

Though. We're due upstairs, to dress—I mean,
To wash our faces. You will forgive us, Madam.

BILLY joins him quickly and both go out, turning as they do and making little bows.

ISABEL:

Turns abruptly and walks to a small table where three leather books are piled. She picks one up, puts it down, then angrily brushes all of them off to the floor.

Animals!

JAGGARD *comes in.*

And you! Why aren't you dressing?

JAGGARD:

Seeing the books and replacing them.

Well, why aren't you? After them both?

Nods toward the door.

ISABEL:

What do you care?

JAGGARD:

                    I *don't* care. That's right.
I'm bored, you're bored, and what each one of us does
Is no concern of the other. That's our system,
And let it be. I merely was diverted:
Two birds, not one, and all in fifteen minutes.

ISABEL:

So far, not in the hand.

JAGGARD:

                    Oh, I'm confident.

ISABEL:

Thank you. Did you drop your little bomb?

JAGGARD:

I did. And he was torn to pieces by it.
At least I think so—hope so. Damn that girl.

ISABEL:

She doesn't know it yet?

JAGGARD:

                    Impossible.
But I shall watch them carefully at dinner.
All evening, too—I'll keep them safely apart.
He said he wouldn't join us; but he will.

ISABEL:

Oh, yes; he went upstairs just now with Warlock.

JAGGARD:

I saw that. Well, then, the thing to do
Is let him boil; the more internal heat
The better. So he mustn't get at her
And blow the lid off—prematurely, I mean.
The best thing, of course, would be for Byrd,
Unable to stand it longer, to rush away.

ISABEL:

Then you'd have *her?* I wonder. She's as gone
On him as you are on her.

JAGGARD:

                                                        Damn her,
Damn her! Why does so much coldness haunt me?
All these months, and not one spark.

ISABEL:

                                                                    You're slipping.

Counts rapidly on both hands.
Think of the females——

JAGGARD:

                                                Think of them yourself.
I don't.

ISABEL:

            Nor I. I'm like you, I don't care.

JAGGARD:

You'd better not. Now, by the way—Warlock.
It wasn't that I cared; but isn't it dangerous?

ISABEL:

How?

JAGGARD:

            A hook in him might tangle things:
Might catch in Mary—Mary—what's her name?

ISABEL:

Scott.

JAGGARD:

   Yes, Scott—might catch in her somehow
And make her blazing mad. Which wouldn't do.
Remember, dearest,

   The epithet, spoken with bitter emphasis, is ironic.

                why we had this party.

ISABEL:

I do, darling.

   With equal irony.

          To strip La Rosa naked.

JAGGARD:

   Impatiently.

But the main thing.

ISABEL:

            Ah, yes. The main thing
Is money, always money, isn't it?

JAGGARD:

Don't be a fool. You know it is. Money's
Your meat and drink.

ISABEL:

            Oh, not my meat.

JAGGARD:

   Shrugs.

                That's men.

ISABEL:

But drink, certainly.

   Pauses.

         Now let me see.

A hook or two in Billy—that might help
To split asunder what God put together.
Those imbeciles, they doubtless think it was God.

JAGGARD:

Go on.

ISABEL:

But Mike—well, I see that.
Considers a moment.

                                                    Yet gently,
Gently, with none but him aware—what harm
In this?

JAGGARD:

       Dangerous, I say.

ISABEL:

                          You doubt
My subtlety. Why, you won't even notice.

JAGGARD:

Go on!

ISABEL:

       The book, the book. I haven't forgotten.
You're paying him to publish it. You're worried
Because so many people don't like war—
These young ones don't, probably—and war's
Your business. So there has to be this book.

JAGGARD:

You put it like a three-year-old. Be serious.

ISABEL:

Laughing.
Author, author!

JAGGARD:

                Damn you!

ISABEL:

You're a father
At last—of four hundred pages. Who's
The mother? Me? No brains.

JAGGARD:

Starts out of the room.

Not one grey cell.

ISABEL:

What would I do with it, poor slippery thing?
But don't you be a fool yourself. I'm serious—
Enough, anyway. My bread, my butter.

She follows him out.

Curtain.

Act Two

The same as Act One, except that the autumn leaves outside are brilliantly floodlighted. It is two hours after dinner.

ISABEL, in evening dress, comes through the door pulling MIKE behind her; he wears the same clothes as in Act One, and seems reluctant to follow her. His face is flushed.

ISABEL:

I wanted you alone, and here we are.
Don't be afraid of me—yet I am dangerous.
I mean, don't be afraid of anything.

MIKE:

His voice a little thick, his speech careful and slow.

Who's afraid?

ISABEL:

I think you are. Or were.

Drops his hand and moves away, her back turned.

I like you in those clothes. I'd like you in any—
None—

262

MIKE:

Wags his finger.

> Now, now!

ISABEL:

Turns at this, laughing in her throat.

> Mike, are you lecturing me?

MIKE:

Goes to her swiftly, unsteadily.

Yes, and the subject is—

Takes her by her bare shoulders and stares at her.

> You're beautiful.

She shakes her head, but tilts it back and smiles.

You are, you are!

Puts his arms suddenly about her and kisses her as she pretends to struggle. At this moment MARY *comes in; but seeing them, stops on her way across the room.*

MARY:

> For God's sake, Mike!

MIKE:

Breaks away but does not turn his head. ISABEL *watches them both as if they were specimens of something.*

> Who's that?

MARY:

Nobody in particular. The old dust rag.

MIKE:

Turns and grins.

Swish, swish.

MARY:

Clenches her hands.

> No, the handle! Oh, but I wish

I had it, and could crack you. Why, you clown,
I'd knock your very ears off—and her eyes.

ISABEL:

Pretty, pretty! You're a *pair* of dolls.
Animated, too.

> *Snaps her fingers at an imaginary servant.*
>> Robert, the camera.

MIKE:

No, she's really mad.

> *Wipes her mouth.*
>> I guess I shouldn't have——

MARY:

Shouldn't. But I didn't dream you *would*.
You've got the right—anybody has—
To be an incredible ass. Only, I thought—

> *Breaks off, half in tears.*

MIKE:

Well, but Neustadt—what have you and he——

MARY:

Neustadt!

MIKE:

> You're his Woman of the Future.
Didn't you think I heard? All through dinner,
And later, by the hour, he carried on
As if you were a piece of modern sculpture,

> *Throws out his arms extravagantly, spastically.*

A mess of shiny metal—rods and curves—
He'd found in some newfangled exhibition.
And how you lapped that up! Didn't you know
I listened? Why, I watched your little tongue
Go in and out—so pleased.

MARY:

The man's a bore.
Everything to him means something else.

MIKE:

And you meant—well, I wonder.

ISABEL:
Archly.

Children, children!

MARY:

Bitch!

MIKE:

Now, Mary.

MARY:

Idiot! Not to see——

Stops as she hears JAGGARD *behind her, knocking both sides of the door with his knuckles as he comes through.*

JAGGARD:

I trust I am intruding.

Smiles without mirth.

Warlock—good!
I wanted you alone, and here you are.

MIKE *looks at* ISABEL *and* MARY *in turn.*

I mean, without the other men. These ladies—
Better still. My wife knows all my secrets.

MARY:

And you hers?

JAGGARD:

I think so. In the long run
It pays.

MARY:

> Unless there is a charge account
> You don't know she's opened.

JAGGARD:

Smiles.

> And you his?

MARY:

> I thought so, till——

JAGGARD:

> Good! You're in the same
> Office, and I dare say you trade
> The latest developments with one another.
> Good! Well, Warlock—remember? I said
> I had a little something to propose.
> What better time than now?

> *Turns away impatiently as* ECCLES, *tipsy, comes in, grace-*
> *fully balancing his steps.*

ECCLES:

> Did you say "time"?
> Ah, there is a time for everything,
> Isn't there, dears? Time is the world's garment—
> Seven veils, they say—and how she wears it
> Is how I know I love her, the old rip.

> *Whirls on the last word, almost falling; but keeps his feet.*

> Ah, she's only a maiden after all.
> No teeth, but a virgin at the heart:
> Deflowered, deflowered—oh, so terribly often—
> Yet still she is a—

> *Waves his hands to catch the word.*

> flower! That's my sweetheart.
> Seven lacy petals make a posy.
> Hear me, darling?

Cups an ear with one hand.

      What did you say? Or sing?
Eat, drink, and be merry, for tomorrow—
What's that, old girl? We die? But *you* won't die.

MIKE:

Maybe this time she will.

ECCLES:

      Did you say "time"?
JAGGARD *goes to take* ECCLES's *arm and lead him away.*

MIKE:

Jaggard, let him be.

  To ECCLES.

      This time, I said.
Neustadt's right, the world does change; and tomorrow
All of us—except, of course, your wrinkled
Mistress—all of us may die. Don't you
Know that?

ECCLES:

     Ah, what a funeral!
Crosses his hands over his chest, then drops them suddenly.

      All of us?

MIKE:

Why not? Consult the military. They're prepared.
Or the arms industry, that keeps us going——

  ISABEL *looks swiftly at* JAGGARD, *who seems not to hear.*

ECCLES:

Going, going, going. What am I bid
For three billion bodies—beautiful bodies—

MIKE:

Ass! They'd stink. And yet no one would smell them.

Even the arms makers—why, they'd stink
Forever, and not a nose would even twitch.
God damn them! Yes, a special stink,
Their stomachs are so full. They're horribly fed.

> ISABEL *clears her throat, trying to get* JAGGARD's *attention, but
> he ignores everybody except* ECCLES, *whom he endeavors
> again to lead out of the room.* ECCLES, *however, jerks himself
> free.*

ECCLES:

To MIKE.

Oh, I know what you mean. A common thought.
There is a time for creation, though, and there's
A time—and why not now—for uncreation?
*De*creation? *Ex*creation? What's
The word? I fumble for it, but it's there.
It's always there

> *Waves his arms before his face.*

                    if you will swim and find it.
There is a time for being and non-being—
Ah, that's better. More euphonious.
Metaphysical, too. Being—being——

JAGGARD:

Seizes ECCLES *roughly and pushes him toward the door.*

You're out of this. You don't belong here, Anson.

Stops, seeing ROSE *about to come in.*

ROSE:

Where's Billy?

Aware of ISABEL, *seems relieved; yet continues.*

                    Anybody know? I've looked
And looked, and I can't find him. He's been strange;
I'm worried.

JAGGARD:

Look some more, my dear. But now—
Please don't mind—we are in conference.

ROSE *looks at* MIKE *and* MARY, *puzzled.*

No matter about what. Not your concern.
As a matter of fact, I saw him in the garden;
You might look there.

ISABEL:

James! Not alone!

JAGGARD:

That's right. Or even at all. It's cold outside.
I'll send a servant.

ROSE:

No, I'll go alone.

Starts for the door.

JAGGARD:

You won't, though. Please!

She stops.

ECCLES:

Eat, drink,
And be merry, for tomorrow we die in the arms—
The arms of—arms, arms—why does that word
Sound so in my ears? Who said it first?

MIKE:

I did.

ROSE:

Laughing nervously.

Arms! But Mr. Eccles, don't
You know?

ECCLES:

　　　　　Darling, I know so much I faint,
I fall.

Pitches forward; recovers.

ROSE:

　But not what Mr. Jaggard does.

JAGGARD:

Rose, my dear, I'll tell him.

ROSE:

　　　　　　　Please let *me.*

To the others.

My boss is modest. He is the great power
Behind—beyond——

ISABEL goes to MIKE and puts a hand on his arm.

ECCLES:

　　　　　Betwixt, between—that's nice.

ROSE:

Beneath, above—but he keeps out of sight—
The industry of arms in this great country.

MIKE:

Strikes ISABEL's hand away.
Great codfish!

MARY:

　　　　So *that's* it!

To MIKE.

　　　　　　We might have noticed—
No one has—the wallpaper. It's human
Skin.

ECCLES:
Shudders.

Ugly! ugly!

MIKE:

So it is.
And those leaves out there, caught on the wire,
Are dripping, dripping blood.

Covers his eyes.

I saw that once
In Germany.

JAGGARD:

Warlock, you're hysterical.

ROSE:

Almost nobody knows. So why not mention it?
Here we are all friends.

ECCLES:

Solemnly.

All, all.

JAGGARD:

Rose, go to your room.

ECCLES:

Aha! He'll follow.

JAGGARD:

Shut up, Eccles.

Touches ROSE'S *elbow; is very courtly.*

My dear, please understand.
All of your remarks are out of order.
Go to your room.

ROSE:

Eluding him.

No. I'll go to the garden.
Poor Billy, he'll be cold.

JAGGARD:

Motions to ISABEL.

Rose! Please!

ISABEL:

Hastening to ROSE.

I'll keep you company. I'll get our wraps——

ROSE:

No, no!

ISABEL:

Yes, Yes. Come with me, silly dear.

ROSE:

Going slowly, speaks mainly to ISABEL.

Poor Billy, he's so jealous. My one cross.
Not here—I don't mean that—

MIKE *turns and looks at* JAGGARD.

Oh, no, at the office.
Nobody's here for him to worry about—
Or there, of course, either. But he loathes
The strange men I smile at every day.
They come and go at my desk like cardboard soldiers—
Nothing to me—I'm nothing to them—but Billy
Says I *receive* them, and that tortures him.
As if my smile meant anything; as if
I ever *saw* them, or were seen by *them*.
He is the only one that really sees me.
I've told him that, I did this morning. But now
Something has got him going again, poor dear.
If it were something different, I'd be glad.
Possibly it is.

ISABEL *nods*.

You think so?

ISABEL:

Know so.

ROSE:

Come on, then.

Takes ISABEL'*s arm.*

We can go different ways—

JAGGARD:

Following to the door and calling through as they disappear.
No, keep together. It is cold and dark.
Isabel, do you hear?

ISABEL:

Offstage.

I do.

JAGGARD:

Returning to the others, preoccupied.

Well, then—
Oh, yes—Warlock. Now I can——

MIKE:

No, you can't.
Not till I tell you something.

MARY:

And I'll help.

JAGGARD:

Don't bother. All of your words I have by heart.
My business is to listen to them daily.
You don't like—what is it?—weaponry.

MIKE:

A fancy word. But no.

MARY:

We don't like it.

JAGGARD:

One of you will be enough.

MARY *stamps her foot.*

Warlock,
How do you think the world has got this far?

MIKE:

How far is that?

JAGGARD:

Well, to wherever it is.

MIKE:

Where is it? Sometimes I can't see. Eccles,
You keep track. Where is the world today?

ECCLES:

Same old place, God bless her; same old shoes;
Same dress; same powder, paint; same simper——

MIKE:

Knock it.

To JAGGARD:

Now you mean, how did the world
Become whatever it is except by battle?
Bang, bang—new growth, new institutions.

JAGGARD:

Nothing like that at all. I simply mean,
How was trouble, when it started, stopped?

MARY:

How could it start? You put a gun in its hand.

JAGGARD:

Stopped or started, how have quarrels been ended?

MARY:

By too many young men having died.

JAGGARD:

Ignoring her.

And as for all that sentimental sorrow,
Well in advance, for the world's end—Warlock,
You can't be one of those.

MIKE:

                 I can. I am.

JAGGARD:

As if measuring him.

In which case—well, it will be harder
To make attractive what I must propose.
I still must, you know.

MIKE:

               For God's sake, Jaggard,
What can it be? Why do you make me wait?

JAGGARD:

All right——

But NEUSTADT *walks in, reading a pamphlet.*

NEUSTADT:

To MARY.

             Miss Scott, see what I found. I was saying—
Remember, after dinner?—this was the important
Subject.

MARY:

            Disarmament, you mean. Yes—

NEUSTADT:

Well, Kirschbaum here is most encouraging.
He proves, I think, we could stop making arms
And still not wreck our vast economy.
A matter, you will agree, of planning—planning
Down to the least detail. First, he remarks

How few of us have seriously considered
The need for this. Convinced of that, we could pool
Our brains—we still have them, in abundance—
Toward the long-wished-for end.

MARY:

Conscious of MIKE.

And may I read it?

NEUSTADT:

Certainly. And Mr. Warlock. All of you.

MIKE:

It's not that new to me. We had a manuscript,
Weeks ago, in the office—Mary, you saw it—

MARY:

Only saw it.

MIKE:

That's the trouble. God,
The madness of the place. It slipped away,
Rejected. I'll admit the man was dull.

NEUSTADT:

Oh, but Kirschbaum isn't.

JAGGARD:

Steps forward.

He is poisonous.

ALL:

What!

JAGGARD:

Pure poison. He is worse than dull;
He's plausible. The nonsense of saying,
As he does, that public works—canals,
Roads, bridges, city halls, and aquaducts—

Would keep the wheels turning. I have studied
How to refute the fool; I've even done so.

MIKE:

What? Have *you* written a book?

JAGGARD:

About to answer, checks himself.

                  So, Neustadt—

NEUSTADT:

Moves nearer to MARY, *who pats his hand.*

Listen. I am a student, as you know,
Of change. I see it everywhere, like snow
That falls in the night and transforms the world.

ECCLES:

The snow, the snow, the beautiful snow.

NEUSTADT:

                        Precisely.

ECCLES:

Imitating him.

Precisely. Thank you, bookkeeper, thank you, thank you.

NEUSTADT:

To me the world is different every morning.

MIKE:

The same breakfast, though.

MARY:

                    Mike, be still.

NEUSTADT:

But the great change is coming.

ECCLES:

Clasping his hands.

Goody, goody.

NEUSTADT:

Greater than any other since the Flood.
Not that I think there ever was a flood,
But it's a convenient reference.

ECCLES:

Ah, yes.

Beckoning.

Come, raven, dove. Come, Ararat.

NEUSTADT:

The rest
Is child's play, compared. This revolution
I mean, my friends, contains within itself
All of the others, as a hen broods
Her chickens, as a father still to be
Is one that will be many. Poverty, greed,
Jealousy, injustice—those are solved
When war is. Eliminate but war,
And every lesser problem solves itself.
This is the great change that I see coming:
So great, I say again——

ECCLES:

Applauding.

Encore, encore!

NEUSTADT:

I say again, so great that *when* it comes
The world we knew will be unrecognizable.
And all because one thing is utterly absent:
War, that children will romance about——

MIKE:

Crouching like a small boy.

Bang, bang, I got you!

NEUSTADT:

               Yes, precisely.

And poets, too, rummaging in the past——

MIKE:

An opening for Byrd. Where *is* our poet?
Page him.

MARY:

          Rose will find him—first, I hope.

That woman—Rose will find him.

MIKE:

                   If he's there.

NEUSTADT:

War will be, my friends, as old-fashioned
As jealousy in lovers, labor unions,
Village greens—as Maypoles, as smallpox.

MIKE:

What a collection. Neustadt, *you're* a poet.

NEUSTADT:

Scarcely.

ECCLES:

Stumbling in a small circle by himself, and singing.

      Here we go round the jealousy tree,

Jealousy tree, jealousy tree. Here we go——

MIKE:

Neustadt, I'd like to think you knew your onions.
It all sounds so easy, though. Some morning
We wake up—is that it?—and snow

Is on the ground—or on your drawing board—
Instead of the war dogs, that died in the night—
Is that it?—and even their carcasses
Have disappeared: dragged to the town dump.

ECCLES:

There is a time for swords, and a time for—sorry!

Bows to an imaginary person.

I pricked you, did I, putting it away?
The scabbard's rusty.

MIKE:

                    Not that I mean, Neustadt,
A disrespect for peace. If you can make it,
Or Kirschbaum can—who's Kirschbaum, anyway?—
I'll order you a monument tomorrow:
The tallest on the continent, for ships
To see from Greenland.

JAGGARD:

                    Neustadt, in my study
There is a book you'll profit now by reading.
A thick, black one: Hammersmith and Harrington.
It's on my desk, holding down some letters.
Don't worry about the letters; find the book
And bring it here, won't you, after a glance
At the Contents? The preface, too—read that.
Take your time. It is a work you'll need
To ponder, as I have. I'll even lend it—
No, I think not, either. Note the publisher,
And get yourself a copy. It will sweep
The cobwebs out. That fantasy of yours!

ECCLES:

As NEUSTADT, *nodding, starts out of the room.*

Wait, Master Slide-rule, wait for Anson.
He wants to go too.

To the others.

                  I dote on libraries:
The old, musty books, with wormholes in them,
And a ladder for the high ones—dusty, dusty!—
Jaggard, I suppose you have a ladder.

JAGGARD:

No such thing. No wormholes, either. All
My books are new, or nearly new. But Anson!
Excellent idea! Go with Neustadt.
And don't hurry back. There is a couch——

ECCLES:

Dear me, no, no. I'd never wake up again.
What was that wine, Jaggard? A book of verses
Underneath the bough——

JAGGARD:

                    No verses.

NEUSTADT:

                    Mary—
If I may call you that—will you come too?

MIKE:

Hastily.

No, she won't. I want her here.

MARY:

                  Oh, do you?
There has to be some woman—is that it?

MIKE:

As NEUSTADT *and* ECCLES *go out.*

Miaou!

MARY:

    Wolf, wolf—Oh!

For ISABEL *comes in, alone.*

                    Where's Billy?

ISABEL:

Not to be found. I left Miss Lynd looking——

JAGGARD:

What did I tell you? Why did you do that?

ISABEL:

Oh, she won't find him if I couldn't.

JAGGARD:

                              Dear,
Go back.

ISABEL:

Shivers.

          It's cold—no. Don't worry, darling.
Moves to MIKE's *side; speaks in a low, quick tone.*
I meant my husband. It's a manner of speech.

MIKE:

In the same tone; but he retreats as she advances.
Approved by all society. Thin blood.

JAGGARD:

Now then, Warlock, we are free at last—
At long last——

MARY:

Covering her ears.
                    Preserve us!

JAGGARD:

                    What?

MARY:

                         From that.
"At long last"!—a phrase I always cut

From anybody's copy. Can't abide it.
So smug, so smeary—oh, it likes itself
All right; but I don't. A long-faced,
Abominable phrase. A vile phrase.

MIKE:

Mary, what a time to pull your rank—
Salutes.
Captain of the copy-cutters, cliché-
Cleavers. Let me listen to mine host.
For all I know, he is about to offer me
A fat job in his infernal factory.

JAGGARD:

To MARY.
I'll do my best not to offend again.
But Warlock, I don't *make* the needful things.
I merely administer—you might say, arrange.

MIKE:

Pimp to the popguns.

JAGGARD:

                    In a way that's true.
Conventional weapons only. As for the others,
The big ones—Government handles those.

MIKE:

With your help, however?

JAGGARD:

Vaguely.
                    Maybe, maybe.

MIKE:

Sure, sure, you mean. But even these,
The sawed-off ones you call conventional—

Damn *them*, I say. They're deadly enough.
They blow holes in brains a bird could fly through.
Or through the guts: a major operation.

JAGGARD:

Men still get hurt, I know. Regrettable.

MIKE:

You don't give a single damn. Regrettable.

JAGGARD:

You don't know that. But listen to me, Warlock.
The book I've written—yes, I've written one—
Presents my case—our case——

MIKE:

                                        A lot of you?

JAGGARD:

Oh, yes, all.

MIKE:

                  In every country?

JAGGARD:

                                        Yes.

MIKE:

I thought so. And that's the worst of it.
If you were simply thinking of our boys,
Our own boys, and how to save their skins,
I'd listen. But Death Incorporated, Death
International—by God, I stop at that.

ISABEL:

Going to MIKE *and slipping her hand under his arm.*
Boy yourself. Impetuous. Now listen.

JAGGARD:

Seeing MARY *bristle.*

My dear, leave it to me.

    ISABEL *does not heed.*

                This book of mine,
Warlock, says it for me. I'm no talker,
But over years I've struggled—and, I think,
Successfully—to put down on paper
The best thought there is upon the subject.

    MIKE:

Thought!

    JAGGARD:

          Yes, thought. Most people merely feel.
You do. She does.

    Nods toward MARY.

    MARY:

    Bitterly.

             You think you know.

    JAGGARD:

I do know. Both of you are typical——

    MARY:

Thanks! The palpitating, pulpy type.

    JAGGARD:

I wouldn't use those words.

    MARY:

          No, only think them.
You're the brainy type. You've written a book.

    JAGGARD:

I have, and that's the business of the evening.
I want your house—and his—to publish it.

    Both stand rigid, speechless. ISABEL *presses herself closer to*
    MIKE, *looking up at him; he does not return the look.*

I want you two to recommend it warmly
To the top decision-makers. Is there still
An Ainsworth? Or do you merely nurse the name?

MIKE:

There is. Fourth generation.

JAGGARD:

      Good. Then Ainsworth—
Go to him and say——

MARY:

      Imagine, Mike!
Sees ISABEL *caressing* MIKE's *arm; runs over and pulls her
away from him so roughly that* ISABEL *staggers, nearly falling.*
As if one Jaggard weren't more than enough.

JAGGARD:

Watching with concern.
Isabel, don't spoil our conference.

MARY:

Jezebel, you mean.

MIKE:

      Mary, be quiet.

MARY:

What? You *want* to hear?

MIKE:

      Not very much.
Still—

JAGGARD:

 The book must stand upon its merit.

MARY:

Merit!

JAGGARD:

If false, the public will say so.
I only want a public.

MARY:

Then you've tried——

JAGGARD:

Yes, everywhere. But publishers are sheep;
They bleat the common message—peace on earth.

MARY:

Do they? Good for them!

JAGGARD:

Which means to me
Confusion. They'll be sorry, as all will,
When danger really comes. I only want
The best ears to listen in the meantime.
The book, once existing, may reach *them.*
That is my only hope—our only hope.

MIKE:

The gentlemen you speak for——

JAGGARD:

They are anonymous.

MIKE:

Then no, Jaggard, no! That's my answer.

JAGGARD:

You haven't heard it all.
Looks hard at MIKE.

You aren't rich?
MIKE *stands rigid again.*
No? Then think of this. There is no limit
To what it's worth to me. You name the figure.

MARY:

A bribe, then.

JAGGARD:

      I don't care what you call it.
We have another name.

MIKE:

Abstracted.

                Doubtless, doubtless.

Alert again.

No, Jaggard, no! To hell with it.

MARY:

That's my boy! Mike, we're going home.
A weekend of this and we'll be nuts.

MIKE:

Mind-reader.

JAGGARD:

      Nonsense. Think it over.
Don't go tonight at any rate. Sleep on it;
Dream; you may wake up a wiser man.

ISABEL:

Suggestively.

Sleep. Dream.

MARY:

      You're out of this—way out.
Be decent, for the love of God.

JAGGARD:

Watching them all.

          Tomorrow,
Then? You'll stay that long? I wish you would.
It never hurts to balance books. And dream.
I spoke of dreaming. It is practical.

Ainsworth, by the way—is *he* rich?
Could *he* dream?

MARY:

Laughing in spite of herself.

A century since he did.
He's old as the Atlantic Ocean. Dream!

JAGGARD:

Well, then, you two. For I mean both of you.
Both of you have books to balance.

MARY:

Me?
I can't add. You wouldn't include me.

JAGGARD:

I would. I do.

MARY:

Think of it, Mike! A heiress!
No, God damn it, no!

MIKE *begins pacing the floor, as if studying the rug.*
You're not *thinking*, are you? What he means
By thought is only fit for a pay-toilet.
He wants you to *feel*,
Pantomime of fondling money.

with dream fingers.
And so does she.

Turns her back on ISABEL, *just in time to see* ROSE *and* BILLY
enter, ROSE *in the lead,* BILLY *following uncertainly.*

Well! And was he singing?
Was that how you found him? In some tree?

ROSE:

Smiling.

Very much on the ground. At the end of the garden.

More serious as she looks back at BILLY, *who does not seem
to know where he should look.*

And silent, silent; he won't say a word.
He looks so strange—what could have happened to him?
Did any of you tell him something horrible?
In fun, perhaps? Not that he wouldn't know.
He likes fun—don't you, Billy?

> *He does not meet her eyes.*

See, people?
He's not himself at all; which is why
I speak of him as if he weren't here.
But *did* you say something—any of you—

> MIKE *looks at* JAGGARD, *who turns away with no expression on his face.*

MARY:

When, for instance? He was glum at dinner;
I noticed that, and tried to catch his eye—
No luck.

> *Laughs.*

Now here I go, like you, discussing——

ROSE:

Oh, that's all right. But I do wonder. Billy,

> *Lowers her voice a little, rejoining him;* JAGGARD *listens closely.*

Here, you know, I'm not a receptionist.
I left my office manners in my desk—
The middle drawer, with the morning and afternoon
Lipstick; and I hung my smile up, too,
On the high hook behind me. No one's here
For you to be jealous of—forgive me, darling,
But I must mention that.

JAGGARD:

> *Speaks with such suddenness that all wheel about to observe him.*

What's this? Jealous?

Neustadt calls it antediluvian.
And so it is—except—
Seems to doubt he should go on, but does.
—except—let's see,
Could *I* be the cause? Could he be jealous
Of *me?*
Snaps his fingers, noiselessly, as if to tell himself he has made a mistake.

ROSE:
As the others stare at JAGGARD.
Of *you!* Please don't joke. It's serious.

ISABEL:
Serious!
Starts laughing.
That's right. James, don't joke.
Her laughter becomes uncontrollable; is hysterical.
Jealous! Of *you?*
Points helplessly at BILLY, *then at* ROSE.
Him? Her? You?
Absurd, absurd! Nobody knows but me
How terribly absurd! A comic book!
Nobody knows but me and *her.*
Points at ROSE *again; almost collapses.*
Of *you,*
She said, of *you!*
BILLY, *unaccountably relaxed, starts laughing also, gently at first, then—with his eyes on* JAGGARD—*uncontrollably in tune with* ISABEL.

JAGGARD:
Isabel, you fool!
Furious, goes over and slaps her hard on both cheeks.
Stop it! Hear me? Stop it!

She obeys like one in a trance, except that a few half-laughs,
half-sobs continue to escape from her.

                    Absolutely—
Now!—stop it!

Quiet again, her shoulders droop. BILLY, *outraged, goes to*
stand beside her.

                    Byrd, leave her alone.
You've been enough trouble as it is.
I don't know what——

     MIKE:

                    You *don't?*

     BILLY:

                              You don't *remember?*

     JAGGARD:

None of that. I say I don't know what
Possessed this woman to be a—spectacle.
You will excuse her, won't you?

Nobody responds.

                    Go to your room,
Darling, and compose yourself.

     ISABEL:

                              I won't.
I'm all right now.

     ROSE:

                    But I don't understand.
I'm sorry, Mrs. Jaggard, if what I said——

     ISABEL:

It was nothing.

     ROSE:

                    Yes, it was; surely it was.

ISABEL:

No, nothing.

ROSE:

> Well, I still don't understand.

BILLY *comes over to her, swiftly, and kisses her.*

There, my sweet! Maybe it doesn't matter.
But when you are unhappy—well, I am.

MIKE:

Striking a pose.

> How I feel
> Is how he does.
> All of our being—
> Buzz, buzz!

BILLY:

Not bad.

MIKE:

> But I was desperate for a rhyme.

ROSE:

Smiling at last.

The second prize—ten dollars—goes to you.

MIKE:

When do I get it?

ROSE:

> When your ship comes in.

To the others.

Now this is more like the way we were.
Billy is happy again. Or I guess he is.

> *Looks up at him and finds him looking at* JAGGARD.

Who knows for sure?

MIKE:

          Perhaps he was being tested.

MARY:

Tested?

MIKE:

    All of us are, all of the time.
And do we pass? Who knows?

MARY:

            Who is the tester?

MIKE:

Next question, please.

MARY:

         Mike, you're crazy.

MIKE:

Well, then, I passed. The clearest sign:
Your girl-friend thinks you're crazy.

MARY:

             Spikka English!

MIKE:

Another sign, not quite so clear: a battered
Head, with bumps and gashes, and one ear—
The left one, as a rule—ready to drop
As soon as the Scotch tape hath lost its stickum.

MARY:

What shall I do with him? He's almost gone.

ROSE:

   Gaily.

If you don't want him, we all do.

MIKE:

             Nobody,
Nobody wants me, and that's fine. I'm flying
Free.

Waves his arms.

Good evening, ladies and gentlemen.

MARY:

But you don't go.

MIKE:

                Why should I, when I like you?
I like you all, I like this place, I like——

MARY:

Mike! You mean——

MIKE:

Mysteriously.

             I mean I think I passed.

Pretends to remove his ear.

Here's this, my duck, to put beneath your pillow.
It makes sweet noises, like an ocean shell.
Or like a watch ticking. Dream away,
My lads, my lassies. Love me, love my left ear.

BILLY:

Beaming.

Warlock, we'll collaborate.

MIKE:

              Aha!
I smell a contract. Beaumont Byrd
And Warlock Fletcher. Ten per cent. OK?

BILLY:

A deal. You do the book, I do the lyrics——

MIKE:

And publish them myself.

Holds his nose.

                    I smell a packrat.

BILLY:

By any other name 'twould smell more sweet.

ROSE:

Whatever all this means—oh, but I'm glad!
Swings BILLY's hand.

MARY:

I think it means Mike is staying for breakfast.

ROSE:

Only breakfast?

MARY:

                    Maybe. That's a lot.

MIKE:

Bowing to ISABEL.
If there's to *be* breakfast.

ISABEL:

Recovered.

                    Yes, of course!

JAGGARD:

His suavity regained, he returns to the center of the room.
Excellent! You're staying then, I take it.

ROSE:

Why, was there any question?

JAGGARD:

                    No, not really.

ISABEL:

We'll have a long table in this room,
With everything on it warming nicely

For when you wander down—oh, any hour.
Breakfast is my specialty. Deep chairs,
With little tables facing them—that's best.
A coffee urn by the window——

MIKE:

I can't wait.
Meanwhile I'll dream.

MARY:

Of rags?

MIKE:

Why not of riches?

JAGGARD:
Why not, why not?
Rubs his hands.

Well, are you people sleepy?
I must confess I am.

MARY:

I am, a little.

MIKE:
Yawns.
I'm already under.

ROSE:

Dear me, now!
I'm wide awake, as if I were five years old
And this was Christmas morning.

MARY:

It isn't that.

ROSE:
I know, it's high October. Look at the leaves!
Goes to the window, stretches luxuriously. All turn and

watch her, motionless, while BILLY, *as the curtain slowly de-
scends, addresses her back.*

BILLY:

> The sun may never rise.
> Something nightly dies.
> Today is not tomorrow;
> The sun may never rise.
>
> Someone said to me—
> Oh, why did I listen?
> Someone said to me—
> Tears glisten.
>
> The moon said to me:
> The stars have all gone out.
> But the sun rose and said:
> Nothing, dear, is dead.

Curtain.

Act Three

<hr />

The same scene the morning after, except that a long table, laden with covered silver dishes, stretches the entire length of one of the walls, and smaller tables stand in front of all the chairs. A tall coffee urn steams at one end of the long table; cups, saucers, silverware, and napkins are conspicuously and conveniently placed.

MIKE comes in, followed by MARY, who watches him go to the long table and lift the covers from several dishes.

MARY:

A person would think you never had seen food.

MIKE:

Rubbing his hands.

I never did—like this. Here, take a look.

She shrugs and turns away.

Honest, now, it's wonderful. Gold eggs.

MARY:

What?

MIKE:

Soft gold, and scrambled.

Lifts another cover.

Boy,
What bacon! From a wild boar, probably.
I wouldn't put it past him—woodcocks, pheasants.

MARY:

We shouldn't have stayed.

MIKE:

Be still.

MARY:

No, we shouldn't.
We could be home by now—in my place, your place,
Cooking as the other half of the world does.
I don't see why this fascinates you so,
She isn't here.

MIKE:

Now, now! And won't be, likely,
Till we are good and gone. I won't take long,
Don't worry. There's a satisfaction, baby,
In robbing them—that's how it feels: absconding
With God knows how many of their calories,
And nothing in return: not even goodbye
And thank you very much—thank you! thank you!

Motions of bowing.

MARY:

But don't you kiss her hand.

MIKE:

Bows very low.

Madame!

MARY:

Runs behind him and pushes him so that he almost falls.

Idiot,

Eat if you must, but don't squat there like that.

Here, I'll get your coffee.

Goes toward the urn, but stops as ROSE *and* BILLY *enter by another door.*

What? You too?

MIKE *turns and sees them; waves.*

We thought we'd be the first.

ROSE:

And so did we.

We never dreamed——

MIKE:

Good morning. But I dreamed——

MARY:

Don't tell them.

ROSE:

Do.

MIKE:

Of infinite riches, lady.

ROSE:

How nice.

MIKE:

Oh, no, it wasn't nice.

ROSE:

I'm sorry.

BILLY:

Midas, were you?

MARY:

                              Yes, he turned hen's eggs
To gold.

MIKE *lifts a cover for them to see.*

ROSE:

Peering in.

       The cook did that. But Billy and I—
We never dreamed we wouldn't be the first.

Stares at them a second.

Now could it be you had the same idea?

MIKE:

For instance.

ROSE:

                    To be gone before *they* came.
But then why should you? We have so much reason,
And you have none at all.

MARY:

                              Oh, no?

ROSE:

                                   I mean—

Looking intently at MARY.

Nothing like what you must have heard. He told you?

Nods toward MIKE.

MARY:

Well, yes, he did. The thing Jaggard said——

ROSE:

That thing.

Shudders.

       Billy has just told *me.*
And so we're leaving.

MIKE:

>Meal ticket and all?

I bow to you—
>*To* MARY.

>>or may I bow?

MARY:

>>>You may,

Sir Mike.
>*To them.*

>>He has the bends this morning.

MIKE:

>>>Billy,

Can you support her? She is on the town.

BILLY:

So far, she has supported me. But now—
Yes, I'll manage.

ROSE:

>>*We* will, *we* will.
>*Breaks down; covers her face.*

>>>Oh,

That thing he said!
>*All are silent for a second, watching her. Then she straightens*
>*suddenly.*

>>But there! I've spoiled your breakfast.

I really am grown up. Such things as that
I know, as you do, are to be expected.

MARY:

From him, you mean?

ROSE:

>>From anybody.

MARY:

                                             But him
Especially?

ROSE:

        From anyone, I said.
Why should I weep for things that are as they are?

MARY:

You were so sweet, I thought; you trusted the world;
You even loved it, maybe, as *he* does.
        Nods toward BILLY.

ROSE:

Oh, not as he does.

MIKE:

                        So you're not a ninny.
Good!

ROSE:

        Don't call him that.

BILLY:

                                Yes, if he likes.
But then he doesn't understand it all.
I even love the evil ones—beginning
With me. I never knew a worse man
Than Billy Byrd.

MIKE:

                        Humility!

BILLY:

                                Not so.
I love whatever *is*, including me;
Which isn't always easy. Now with Rose
It is, for Rose is perfect.

ROSE:

Her voice breaking briefly.

Crazy man!

BILLY:

The rest of the world—well, I see its evil
As something that belongs there, and I love it
Simply because it is. A distant view
Is better, of course——

MIKE:

Aha!

BILLY:

And so I take
As many backward steps as I do forward.
This morning, for example. I am leaving—
Both of us are—Jaggard and his lies.
I love even those; but I don't like them.
They aren't mine. I am a liar too.
I never knew a worse one.

MIKE:

Rub it in,
That's right. If this isn't humility,
What is, I want to know? Neustadt, now—
He'd say it was old-fashioned; out of phase,
Or some damned thing like that. Mary my girl,
You know him better than I do; how would he put it?

MARY:

Making a face.

Pooh!

BILLY:

Old-fashioned? No, it's necessary
If one's not to go mad.

MIKE:

Don't poets want that?

BILLY:

No. You know they don't.

MIKE:

There's help, then.

BILLY:

There always is. But anyway, we're leaving.
A little distance is the thing we need
Between us and his lies.

MIKE:

So they *were* lies.

ROSE:

Yes, lies. Do you mind if I sound virtuous?
I am old-fashioned. I am single-minded.
There's nobody but Billy, and never was.

BILLY:

You see? Perfect.

ROSE:

Quiet, quiet! And no one
Knows this better than him I used to work for.

MARY:

Used to?

ROSE:

Looks away.

Years ago.

MIKE:

The death of time.
Eccles ought to be listening—his subject.

Goes to the long table and helps himself to breakfast, which as he talks he takes to the deepest chair and commences eating.

Eccles loves time. He even likes it.

Grins at BILLY.

And so do I, if it has brought this change
That Neustadt never dreamed of.

BILLY:

                                    Neustadt? Dream?

MIKE:

The man does nothing else. Or does he, Mary?

MARY:

Making a face again.

Fasten your bib. Careful, now, don't spill.

ROSE:

Jaggard tried and tried. He never gave up
Trying—every way that men do.

MIKE:

You know them all?

ROSE:

                     Who doesn't?

MARY:

                            Yes, she's right.

ROSE:

He tried so hard, and got nowhere so fast—
And yet it seemed slow, too—so dreary—
That in the end he simply hated me.
I'm sure of that. He did his worst then
To hurt me. And he almost did.

MARY:
Goes to her.

My dear!

ROSE:
Not quite, because you both——

MARY:

What did *we* do?

ROSE:
You were my friends. I was at home with you.
No matter what you said, I was at home.

MARY:
That's nice.

MIKE:
That's very nice.

ROSE:
Don't be embarrassed.
You don't have to say a single thing—
A pause, while MIKE *eats his toast noisily.*
Or do a single thing. It was enough,
It is enough, that both of you are here.
For one thing, I wanted you to know
How hard the man tried, and why therefore
He hated me.

BILLY:
The woman. Now I wonder
If Isabel—is that her name?—hates *me.*
Last night she tried to tuck me in.

MIKE:
Almost chokes on a bite.
My God,
You too? I thought I was the only one.

She slipped in to see if I was comfortable—
Something about pillows, or the window—

MARY:

But certainly, the bitch!

MIKE:

Waving his fork at her.

                              Language, language!
Well, I was—
Grins at ROSE.
                what do you call it? Old-fashioned.
So——

MARY:

    So?

MIKE:

Picks pieces off his toast and drops them.
          Hate me, hate me not.

ROSE:

They hate us all, I'm sure. Yet in your case—
Mary, Mike—I wonder why, apart
From the tucking in: routine, I'd say, with her,
So that can't be the reason. I haven't asked—
Forgive me—why you two are skipping out.
I am the one that has to be told of things;
I've been sleepwalking.
    A silence.
                    Mary, was it you?
Did Jaggard——

MARY:

                Lady, he hath been true to thee.
He hardly knows I'm here.

BILLY:

                    He knows Mike is.

MIKE:

I think he does.

BILLY:

               Well, then——

MIKE:

                         Out with it, Byrd.

BILLY:

A man's been known—more and more it happens——

MIKE:

Ho, ho! So you do know your way around.

BILLY:

Embarrassed.

Forgive me, but it crossed my mind.

MIKE:

                         A filthy

Mind?

BILLY:

    I hope not.

MIKE:

               Good. But even so,

Your guess was not so wrong. He has designs—

Oh, yes—and they are worse than you'd imagine.

    To ROSE.

I have a better reason to be gone

Even than you have, and you've got a good one.

ROSE:

How could this be?

MIKE:

           I only know it is.
Listen. Do you really want to hear it?

ROSE:

Of course, of course. If I had any illusions,
All of them were shattered by his lie.
But then I had none. It was hell enough
To work for such a man—I mean, a man
Who does what he does. I was slow in learning—
Jaggard is sly; his business is top secret—
But when I did, why did I stay there?
I know—so Billy and I would never starve.

BILLY:

You didn't tell me that.

ROSE:

              Of course not, dearest.
And now we will.

BILLY:

          We won't.

MIKE:

              Children, children.
Whatever it is, you'll do it both together.
We all know that.

ROSE:

To MIKE.

          Tell me, then.

MIKE:

             Oh, yes.
Jaggard. He wants to make me a rich man.

BILLY:

What?

MIKE:

Oh, I exaggerate. And so
Does Jaggard. When the time comes he'll jingle
Silver in the bottom of his money-bags.
He'll welch.

ROSE:

But answer Billy, please. What *is* it?

MARY:

Dear, it isn't simple. So fantastic!

MIKE:

That's right, fantastic. For a man like him—
Practical, presumably—to believe
The whole deal would make an ounce of difference.
As if one book could change the world—his, anyway.
Not that I've seen it; nor do I intend to.

ROSE:

Throwing up her hands.
Please, Mike!

MIKE:

OK, I'll shoot. Your boss, then,
Has written a book. And for a consideration—
No limit there, he says, but that's a lie—
I'm to recommend it to *my* boss.

ROSE:

What kind of book?

MIKE:

About the good of war—
The blessing of big weaponry—the need
For all of us who hate the god damned things
To love them suddenly; to leave his gang
Alone that makes and sells them, and—he says—
Saves us. We're in danger, and they save us.

ROSE:

A bribe, then.

MIKE:

    Oh, yes. To me and Mary.

MARY:

A heiress I'm to be.

Rotates like a mannikin.

     See my diamonds?

MIKE:

And even to my boss. The sky's the limit.
Fantastic—that's the word.

ROSE:

      Yet he may mean it.

Droops.

The worst thing is, he does! Oh, my God,
That I am still with him—or I was
Till yesterday—this morning. I'm ashamed.

BILLY:

Sweetheart——

ROSE:

    I'm ashamed.

Pause; then turns fiercely to MIKE.

      What will you do?
What will you say? Don't think he doesn't mean it.
No limit—that's no lie. You can't conceive
The depth of what you call his money-bags.
Silver at the bottom? No, Mike,
It's paper, and it crackles. Gilt-edged.

MIKE:

Returning to the long table with his plate.

I'm going to have more sausages. Quite the finest
I ever sunk a fang in. All you people—
Why don't you eat? It's here. Breakfast's the great
Meal of the day.

MARY:

It's all for you, giant.
Go on, and we'll just listen—

Covers her ears.

—munch, crunch.

ROSE:

As MIKE *returns to his chair.*
But what have you decided?

MIKE:

Wags his head.

Think of asking.
I'll tell you this, though. If the man comes in
Before I'm finished you will hear a speech.
That will be clear enough.

ROSE:

Then I can guess.

MIKE:

Can you?

ROSE:

To begin with, you are waiting
Until he does come in. You could have gone——

MARY:

I wanted to. But now I know I don't.
You're right, dear, we're waiting.

ROSE:

So am I.

BILLY:

And I. Unfinished business.

MIKE:

> Poet and pugilist.

Got your brass knuckles handy? So you're waiting.

ROSE:

Yes, and without knuckles. Words, though.

BILLY:

Musing.

Words.

MIKE:

> Good. I'll listen.

ECCLES *comes in quietly and goes to the long table.*

> Meanwhile, here's

An audience. Try them on Eccles. Eccles, old man,
What time of the world is it? There is a time
For good eggs, wouldn't you say? And there is a time
For rotten ones?—whew!

Holds his nose.

ECCLES:

Lifting the covers and sniffing the contents.

> Till I've had breakfast

I never talk. I don't even say good morning.
I don't smile, either. There is a saying:
"Sing before breakfast, cry before night." I'm dead
Till noon, really.

MIKE:

> Eccles, you're always dead.

MARY:

Shshsh!

MIKE:

     Oh, but he is. What does he know?
What do you know, Eccles—I mean for certain?
Nothing! What you call your brain is mush,
Is fungus: moldy stuff about the way
The world goes—old girl, you call her. Old
Indeed. You're pure corruption—or impure,
And probably contagious. When we go
We'll breathe good air again: young air.
You're shapeless, too: a bag of wornout feathers
That bulges this way, that way, as the pressure
Is felt of those about you. You agree
With everybody; but the vilest, most.
Jaggard, for instance—ah, his famous dinners,
His infamous foul thoughts. Eccles——

ROSE:

                        Mike!
I wouldn't have dreamed that you could be so cruel.

ECCLES:

Who has never looked up.

Thank you, dear.

ROSE:

To MIKE.

          He is the nicest man.

MIKE:

Nonsense. He's a menace. So is *he*.

As NEUSTADT *enters.*

What does *he* really know?

     NEUSTADT, *cool and brisk, greets them all and goes to the*
table; but stops and turns.

NEUSTADT:

                What did you say,

Warlock, if it's any of my business?
Was it about me?

MIKE:

You bet it was.
I said—or I will say—that you're all tape
And ticker. You've got celluloid for brains.
The world for you is paste, is plastic, gum—
Bubble gum, by God, for you to pop.
You don't believe a thing, or see a thing,
Any more than Eccles does. You're useless.

MARY:

Mike, you're mad—what have you swallowed, darling?
Remember? Mr. Neustadt prophesied
The end of war on earth. So he believes
One thing you do.

MIKE:

He doesn't. It's a game
He plays—whisk, and the blueprints prance.
It isn't real for him. He isn't angry.
Show me that he cares, and I'll shut up.

NEUSTADT:

Deftly and efficiently, while MIKE *harangues, collecting his
breakfast and arranging it on a small table before him.*

Warlock,

He beheads an egg.

something is different here this morning.
There has been change. I feel it, smell it, taste it——

MIKE:

Good. So you have senses. *Do* you, though?
One change in me, if you must know, is this:
That speech of yours last night was less than nothing.
I didn't think so then; I do so now.
You think peace is coming by itself:

Developed on a plate in someone's darkroom—
Your own, I suppose. Well, listen to me.

NEUSTADT:

Gladly, if you won't be personal.

MIKE:

There! That's it! Personal—why not?

NEUSTADT:

More heat than light. I am for light.

MIKE:

Raises his hands and crosses them.

                                        Mazda!
But these things are personal or nothing.

NEUSTADT:

What things?

MIKE:

                    I meant to tell you. All of us four
Have changed our minds. We are not staying here;
The weekend is over.

NEUSTADT:

Looking at him over his glasses.

                              Very interesting.

MIKE:

Not to you. Nothing is. Nothing!

NEUSTADT:

I mean, that you have changed your minds. On principle
I approve. The changing of one's mind——

MIKE:

One's! What a woozy word! One's old T-shirt,
One's smelly socks.

NEUSTADT:

   Those too.

MIKE:

     Listen, four-eyes——

MARY:

Mike! What has he *done*, what has he *said*,
To make you talk this way?

ECCLES:

Putting down his coffee cup.

      Don't listen, Neustadt.
He only will insult you—if he can.

MIKE:

The silent man sounds off, though it isn't noon yet.

ECCLES:

Disregarding him.

The mind, don't you know, changes itself.
It has its own career within the skull,
And only our vanity says we control it.
Within the skull, I say; but where for certain
Is it? I don't know. Some days I see it
Naked, like the head of John the Baptist,
Bleeding on a platter: bleeding thoughts
And feelings that are old as the first man,
Yet still they ooze and flow, forever
Fresh, forever wonderful—a heart,
Perhaps; or no, a pomegranate, staining
The whole room bright red.

  ROSE *and* MARY *are half fascinated, half horrified.* MIKE
  throws up his hands.

MIKE:

     There you are!
Corruption: rotten fruit.

BILLY:

                              A handsome image,
Eccles. I'll remember it, and use it—
May I?

ECCLES:

    Thought is free.

BILLY:

                      Thank you.

ECCLES:

                                  And so's
Imagination. You are welcome.

BILLY:

                              Thank you.

ECCLES:

Don't say that. It is no longer mine.
Having escaped me, it is yours—and yours—
    Waving to the others.

MIKE:

Thank you, I don't want it.

ECCLES:

                          Just as you please.

BILLY:

Stepping toward ECCLES *and* NEUSTADT *in turn.*
But Mike didn't tell you. Things have happened—
Things outside of us—to change our plans.
It isn't merely that the pomegranate——

NEUSTADT:

What has happened?
    A silence.

                          Now I should have said
That to this hour

Looks at his watch.

>   the weekend has been—
What shall I say?—singularly uneventful.

MIKE:

Say that. It sounds like you.

BILLY:

As the JAGGARDS, *all smiles, sweep in.*

>   Now you'll see.
He and MIKE *do not move; but* ROSE *and* MARY *withdraw
toward one corner of the room, and* ECCLES *and* NEUSTADT
rise, standing by their tables.

JAGGARD:

Keep your seats, gentlemen.
>   *They sit down.*

>   Warlock,
Good morning.

>   MIKE, *from his chair, soberly salutes.*

>   But the rest of you—
Turns to them; they do not respond.

>   —proceed
With breakfast, which I see you haven't started.
Perhaps you just came down. We got up late
Deliberately, to let you be alone here.
There's nothing like a host to spoil an egg.
Isabel, the ladies may be waiting
For *you.*

>   ISABEL, *seeing that they still do not respond, waits.*

>   Well, Mr. Byrd, at least join *me.*
There's everything, for every taste. And coffee—
Ah, I shouldn't praise ours, but I do.
You may not know the secret: cold water
Dripping through and through it, over and over,
All night—yes, all night, the Java way—
Then heated just before it's carried here.

Looks from one to another.
What is it, friends? Why are you not at ease?

MIKE:

Pushing his table away from him, but keeping his seat.
Jaggard, you are right about the breakfast.
The coffee, too. I never tasted better.

JAGGARD:
Uncertainly.
Good, good.

MIKE:

But this is not so good:
Four of us are leaving right away.
Stands up.
You know which four I mean:
Counts on his fingers.

Mary, me,
Rose, Billy.

JAGGARD:
Flushing.
This is preposterous!

BILLY:
Oh, no, it isn't.

JAGGARD:
Let Warlock tell me why.

MIKE:
Jaggard, you know. Please don't play innocent.
It's sickening.

JAGGARD:
Well, then—

MIKE:

           That's better. Rose,
Wouldn't you rather be the first to tell?

ROSE:

I'll wait.

MIKE:

      Or Billy?

BILLY:

        Thank you, I'll wait too.

MIKE:

Your proposition, Jaggard, didn't improve
With sleep. In fact, it stank all night beside me
And wouldn't let *me* sleep. I threw it out
This morning—slop!—your gardener will find it
Withering the chrysanthemums. Your book
Will never, if I can help it, reach one reader.
Far from accepting the fat bribe you offer,
I'll spend my own money, such as it is,
To lunch with publishers, and let them know
What wolf is running wild in the tall canyons.
That's you, Jaggard, you. The book is dead.

JAGGARD:

To NEUSTADT.
A publisher, and he would kill a book.

NEUSTADT:

It isn't clear to me——

MIKE:

        Of course it isn't.
But I don't think you'd care.

JAGGARD:

        A free press,
With every publication taking its chances——

MIKE:

Free, my foot! You'd pay me to deceive
My own boss, and Mary's.

MARY:

Poor old Ainsworth.

MIKE:

Jaggard, didn't I make it plain last night?

JAGGARD:

You told me you would sleep on it—and dream.

MIKE:

Shaking his head as if to clear it.

Nightmares, Jaggard, nightmares!

JAGGARD:

I am flattered.

Isabel, *I* gave this boy a night
He never will forget.

She looks between them, unsmiling.

MIKE:

And so I won't.

JAGGARD:

So much result from one poor book, unread.

NEUSTADT:

Please let me understand. He kills a book
He hasn't read?

MIKE:

A book in praise of war.
A book no other publisher will print,
And so he offers me a pot of money——

NEUSTADT:
Meditating.
. . . War . . .

MIKE:

        The thing you said last night was finished—
Or would be—or should be.

NEUSTADT:

                So I did.

MIKE:
Well?

NEUSTADT:

   And you've not read it.

MIKE:

              No.

JAGGARD:

                  You see?
I want a public, and will pay for one—
That's all. He calls it bribery.

NEUSTADT:

              How so?

MIKE:
Very simple. I'm to recommend it
When no one else would in this cockeyed world;
And for that little deed I write my own
Check—you understand?—in any amount.
Is that corruption, Neustadt? What do you say?

NEUSTADT:
Abstracted.
Hmm. Perhaps a new definition
Is needed of the term. Perspectives shift

And imperceptibly alter with the changing
Times.

MIKE:

To MARY, *holding his hands out, palms up.*

  There! You wondered——

MARY:

Runs to him, outraged.

          I was wrong,
Mike. Now come! We're through with them *all* for good.
Let's go.

NEUSTADT:

  But Mary——

MARY:

         Scott to you. Miss Scott.

NEUSTADT:

I only meant——

MARY:

      Nothing. And *mean* nothing.
Come on, Mike, for God's sake.

Putting out a hand.

         Rose—Billy——

ROSE:

Wait. Mr. Jaggard—*James* Jaggard—
As of this moment I am unemployed.

JAGGARD:

As if nothing could surprise him.

Unemployed? Or unemployable?
Remember, I have influence. You will starve.

BILLY:

Taking a step toward him.

No, she won't. You'd like to think so.

JAGGARD:

                                        Why,

I *love* the thought. You, too—for what can *you* do?
Peddle verses? Try that in Wall Street.
But Rose, in all seriousness, enlighten me.
This is so sudden, as they used to say.
Are you like Warlock all at once—shocked,
As he is? Are you taking sides against me?
I never forgive treachery, you know.

ROSE:

I am ashamed ever to have been
Your servant in that place. But more than this,
I know—we all know—what you said last night
To him, and him, and him, and *him*.

    Pointing in turn to MIKE, ECCLES, NEUSTADT, BILLY.

                                You lied,

And all of us believe you lied. I learned
Only this morning—half an hour ago—
How terribly, how brutally, you lied.

JAGGARD:

Looking particularly at ECCLES *and* NEUSTADT.

I see. So they have taken your bare word.
Or have they?

MARY:

Stamping both feet.

            Hog!

MIKE:

            Language, language!

MARY:

You—

Language!

JAGGARD:

The bare word, I say, of one
Concerning whose behavior there might be—
Will be, I swear it—witnesses.
I didn't lie last night. Go if you please,
I'm through with you; but what we once were——

BILLY:

Comes at him with fists raised.

I'll kill you, Jaggard!

ROSE:

Screams.

Billy!

He stops; lowers his hands.

Let him be.
Don't touch him. He is pitch, and he'll come off
As black as night all over both of your hands.

Turns to ISABEL.

You, too; though no one thinks of touching *you*.

ISABEL:

I don't know what you mean.

ROSE:

So innocent,
Like him. You are a pair. I wish I knew
How you two talk together when you're alone.

ISABEL:

You never will.

ROSE:

> Of course not. Thank God

For that, at least.

MARY:

> Small favors. Ask for more.

Ask that we'll forget this hideous party.

MIKE:

No, sweet. Necessary to remember.

> *Starts away, beckoning for the other three to follow.*

We learn about life little enough
Most days; so when it rises up and hits us

> *Dodges like a boxer.*

We take it and we put a ticket on it:
Remember this.

JAGGARD:

> Thank you.

To ECCLES *and* NEUSTADT.

> Gentlemen,

Be witness to the impression I have made—
I and my dear wife—

> *Bows to* ISABEL, *who only stares at him.*

> upon these infants.

They aren't of this world. We thought they were,
But look, they run like mice.

NEUSTADT:

> Angry, angry.

The first thing I noticed in them.

MIKE:

> Neustadt,

You haven't got it in you to be angry.
I knew that right away. And as for Eccles——

ECCLES:

There is a time for wrath, there is a time——

MIKE:

Click clock.

Leans down, his hand behind his ear.

　　　　　Do you hear Grandmother Earth?

Stands and looks at ECCLES.

She's that man's mistress, and she ticks away
Like a gold watch in cotton deep down there.

ECCLES:

Excellent, Warlock! But as I was saying,
There is a time not to be angry, too.
Not to be self-righteous, not to be—
Permit me—young.

MIKE:

　　　　　Well said, my ancient mushroom,
Liquefying horribly in the sun:
All brown, all slimy, with black ants acrawl.

ECCLES:

Now who's the poet here?

MIKE:

　　　　　Oh, Billy is.
And by the way, he said he loved the lies
Of others like his own—listen, Jaggard,
He did say that, not long before you came;
But *when* you came he wanted to kill the one
Liar who is eminent among us—you.
Billy, do you love him now?

BILLY:

　　　　　Yes.

MIKE:

Hey! No double talk.

BILLY:

But at a distance.

Rose reminded me.

MIKE:

And rescued *him.*

JAGGARD:

Shall I be grateful?

ROSE:

No. You haven't the art.

ECCLES:

That's good. I don't mean true. But it was good,
What the girl said. Art—ah, that's the thing.

ISABEL:

Mr. Eccles, you are a silly man.

All, surprised to hear her speak, turn her way.

ECCLES:

I like that too. It is my role.

ISABEL:

Be quiet.

I wasn't paying you a compliment.

ECCLES:

Taken down.

Oh, dear.

ISABEL:

Now I will show these others out.

MARY:

Drawing apart from her.

We know the way.

ISABEL:

If distance is what you want,
You'll have it, by the nearest door of several.
Come, I'll show you which.

The four young people look at one another as she walks past them.

Quickly now!

JAGGARD:

Isabel, stay here.

ISABEL:

No, darling, I think not.
Failure bores me.

JAGGARD:

Laughs, a little nervously.

What?

ISABEL:

Mine, too.

MIKE:

Bowing.

Now, Madam——

ISABEL:

No more words.

MARY:

Puzzled, but impressed.

Thank you, even?

ISABEL:

No.

They hesitate again, looking toward JAGGARD, who avoids their eyes. Then MARY puts her arm around ROSE's waist, MIKE lays his hand on BILLY's shoulder, and the four of them start moving after ISABEL. But they stop abruptly as MIKE turns back.

MIKE:

I still have a lot to say.

MARY:

Running to him.

Don't say it.

MIKE:

Pushing her off.

Only this, then. I am glad I came,
Just as I'm glad I'm going. Billy is right.
Terrible as you are, we love you all——

MARY:

What!

MIKE:

—because you helped us love ourselves
At least a little better. It's too soon
To be dead sure, but Warlock is a friend
I think I've made for life.

Shakes hands with himself.

Good old Warlock!
Howdy, boy! Keep talking as you did
Last night and now this morning. I enjoyed it,
Really I did. We can get on together.
And so,

Bowing to the three older men, and then to ISABEL, impatient at the door.

with ceremony we depart.
There *must* be ceremony. Thank you, thank you.

> *Bows again, but is almost pulled off his balance by* MARY,
> *who jerks him into his former position. The four now follow*
> ISABEL *through the door; though she reappears in it after a*
> *few seconds.*

ISABEL:

I shall see all three of you at lunch;
Not before.

ECCLES:

      Me, too?

ISABEL:

          Certainly.
But don't ask me to remember things.
I loathe remembering things, and being asked
Whether I meant something I once said.

> *Goes out, and a long silence ensues.* ECCLES *and* NEUSTADT
> *stare straight before them;* JAGGARD *walks slowly, softly,*
> *back and forth, his eyes on the thick rug that muffles his*
> *steps.*

NEUSTADT:

Remarkable.

> *Another silence.*

ECCLES:

      Humiliating, rather.

JAGGARD:

> *Stops pacing.*

You mean the thing my wife said to you?
That was for their benefit. Somehow
She thought she had to soothe them, there at the end.
And it did get them out. I'll ask her later.
Meanwhile I'll confess that it surprised me.

ECCLES:

No, not merely what she said that time,
Though it did take me back a bit. I mean,
Jaggard, the whole thing, the terrible *taste*
Of it, or *lack* of taste. This generation——

NEUSTADT:

Remarkable.

More silence.

ECCLES:

       A faint word, Neustadt,
If I may say so.

NEUSTADT:

        No, precisely right:
Remarkable. I should have taken notes;
And shall, when I get home.

Pauses.

              When will that be?
Jaggard, shouldn't we go too? The party
Is over that you planned. Your wife meant this
By "failure," I presume; her own and yours.

JAGGARD:

Yes.

Starts pacing again, then stops.

No! Forget that. It was for me.
I can't explain, nor do I care to. Don't
Go, however. Anson, you must stay.

ECCLES:

Forever, more or less. I mean, of course,
Through Sunday.

NEUSTADT:

       Then I will.

ECCLES:
Wickedly.

                                    The notes, though.

NEUSTADT:
I have a desk here in my room.

JAGGARD:

                                    Use it.
No one else has.

ECCLES:

                    How I'd like to see them!
Motions of note-taking.
"Mary Scott: a hitherto unencountered
Specimen of"—what, I wonder? "Mike Warlock:
Angry!"—that, of course. "William Byrd"—
Don't say "Billy." It's ridiculous.
In Shakespeare's time there was a William Byrd:
A cunning musician; he wrote madrigals.

NEUSTADT:
Thank you; I'll remember. That was before
Poetry died.

ECCLES:

                    Did it? I would say,
A time when people studied how to write it—
And sing it, too. They learned it and they lived it.
Well—oh, yes: "Rose Lynd"——

JAGGARD:
Clearing his throat.

                                    Gentlemen,
I'll eat my breakfast now, and then if you like
We'll walk a little about the grounds; I have
Extraordinary things to show my guests.
I always do, and they are always pleased.

NEUSTADT:

Miss Lynd——

JAGGARD:

            For instance, the chrysanthemum house.
It rivals, I may say, the famous ones
In Boston and New York.

NEUSTADT:

                 Miss Lynd——

JAGGARD:

                        And then
The stables. I have trotters; one I drive
Myself, at the August meets.

NEUSTADT:

                You spoke of witnesses——

JAGGARD:

Damn you! Can't you see——

ECCLES:

                 Postpone the topic,
Neustadt.

NEUSTADT:

       I *can* see. But then the book.
Jaggard, may I read it while I'm here?

JAGGARD:

Startled; studies NEUSTADT's *face.*

Warlock has conditioned you against it.

NEUSTADT:

No one can do that. I have as free
A mind as any living man.

ECCLES:

                    Ho, ho!
You're certain it's your own?

NEUSTADT:

                    Quite, quite certain.

ECCLES:

Congratulations. Mine is a ball of thread
That winds, unwinds by devious devices—
So strange those are! I dote on them.

NEUSTADT:

                    No doubt.

JAGGARD:

A free mind, you say. I won't inflict
My pages on you here and now; but Warlock's
Mind is *not* free; he is prejudiced.
Nor did he ever listen when I spoke
Of any reader's liberty to reject,
Or modify, or simply, in a calm hour,
Consider. I would pay for such an audience;
And Warlock, having found it, would be free
For life to work as little as he pleased.

NEUSTADT:

Yet he elected otherwise.

JAGGARD:

                    He did.

NEUSTADT:

Remarkable.

JAGGARD:

Snapping his fingers as he turns away.
                    Confound it, can't you change
That record you are playing?

ECCLES:

It *is* tedious.

NEUSTADT:

Is it?

Stirs in his chair.

I shall not apologize—
Except for going when I said I'd stay.

JAGGARD:

Wheels back.

What's that?

NEUSTADT:

Standing up slowly.

I'm going to see if I can find them—
Those four—and put to them a list of questions
I couldn't ask when they were overwrought.

Pauses.

They are so old—as of another time—
That I am lost among them. Youth, I thought,
Had put behind it everything these cherish:
Poetry, indignation, loathing, love,
And—most remarkable of all—fidelity.
It is as if their grandsires lived in them,
Ignoring every novelty since Adam,
If Adam ever was; and now I wonder.
They are old-fashioned, being natural:
A thing I thought had no place in our time.
Yet here it is, and I must see it closer.

JAGGARD:

Neustadt, you're a numskull.

ECCLES:

Can you *find* them?
And if you ever do, will they abide you?

Remember how they talked—or Warlock did,
And Mary Scott consented. They don't like you.
Me, either—*I* remember. I'll avoid them.
And that won't be hard. Whoever sees them?

NEUSTADT:

I can. I will.

To JAGGARD.

                    Good morning, sir, and thank you.

Offers his hand, which JAGGARD *appears not to see.*

Eccles, you don't send them your regards,
I take it.

ECCLES:

Rolling his eyes upward.

          Heavens above me, no!

NEUSTADT:

                              Well, then—
Oh, yes, Jaggard. My compliments to your wife.
Please thank her for me too.

JAGGARD *is silent.*

                    Well, then——

ECCLES:

                              Goodbye,
Neustadt. I hope their answers will be serious.

NEUSTADT *goes out stiffly, without once looking back. A
silence ensues as* ECCLES *watches* JAGGARD *resume his pacing
of the rug.*

They may refuse to see him.

JAGGARD *shrugs.*

                    He's pathetic.

JAGGARD:

At last.
So are you.

ECCLES:

Dear, dear!

JAGGARD:

Don't be offended.

ECCLES:

Touching, you may mean. I trust I am touching.

JAGGARD:

That's it. You are.

ECCLES:

Thank you. Pity is sweet.

JAGGARD:

Is it? Most of the people I know resent it;
Some of them with fury.

ECCLES:

Poor people!
So charming to be pitied. I can pity
Myself when no Samaritan is by
To do it for me.

JAGGARD:

Eccles, you're an odd one.

ECCLES:

Only because I'm frank, as you can be;
I never object to frankness.

JAGGARD:

What do you mean?

ECCLES:

Failure's to be pitied.

JAGGARD:
Stops dead.

Failure?

ECCLES:

Richly intoning the word.

Failure.

Waits a second.

Yours. And hers—your beautiful wife's. Her word.

JAGGARD:

You didn't hear it.

ECCLES:

Ah, but I did.

JAGGARD:

His throat tightening.

Be careful!
You didn't hear it; there was no such word.
I haven't failed. As for my wife—listen!
Leave her alone. And as for me——

ECCLES:

Be frank,
Be honest.

JAGGARD:

Damn you! Eccles, you can't dream
Of what I may do—will do—must do—yet.

ECCLES:

Musingly.

Perchance to dream.

JAGGARD:

No poetry now. Byrd's
Was more than enough.

ECCLES:

Byrd. I heard him saying

This to himself last night when he was alone,
Or thought he was. There was music, too: from the fountain.

> *The curtain slowly descends as he recites, and as* JAGGARD,
> *apparently not listening, goes to the table for his breakfast.*

Dark of the world,
With day inside,
Tell me: where
Doth sweetness hide?

Night of the soul,
Away from the sun,
Say to me: where
Is my sweet one?

Worm and thorn,
With death in your bite,
Is nevertheless
All well tonight?

Yes, sir, yes, sir.
Sleep till morning.
Even now
The birds are returning;
With dew on the rose
For her adorning.

Curtain.